HOW TO DRINK
WINE

HOW TO DRINK WINE

13-Digit ISBN: 978-1-40034-060-6
10-Digit ISBN: 1-40034-060-8

This book may be ordered by mail from the publisher. Please include $5.99 for postage and handling. Please support your local bookseller first!

Books published by Cider Mill Press Book Publishers are available at special discounts for bulk purchases in the United States by corporations, institutions, and other organizations. For more information, please contact the publisher.

Cider Mill Press Book Publishers
"Where good books are ready for press"
501 Nelson Place
Nashville, Tennessee 37214
cidermillpress.com

Typography: Knockout, Trade Gothic

Image Credits: Page 4 by Rowan Heuvel on Unsplash. Pages 6–7 by Dan Cristian Padure on Unsplash. Page 77 by Corina Rainer on Unsplash. Page 95 by Sven Wilhelm on Unsplash. Page 220 by Ira Pavlyukovich on Unsplash. Pages 222–223 by Tim Mossholder on Unsplash. All other photos courtesy of the author.

Printed in the United States of America

24 25 26 27 28 VER 5 4 3 2 1

First Edition

HOW TO DRINK
WINE

CARLO DEVITO

FROM GRAPES TO GLASSES, EVERYTHING YOU NEED TO KNOW

CIDER MILL
PRESS

BOOK
PUBLISHERS

CONTENTS

PROLOGUE

Back in 2014, I was talking with my friend Richard Leahy, the author of *Beyond Jefferson's Vines*, about some of our favorite wineries in the state of New Jersey, among other things. And I reminisced that one of my favorite wineries, for sentimental reasons, was Cream Ridge Winery. That was when Richard told me that the owner, Tom Amabile, had recently passed away. I paused. It was like someone had slapped me.

When I was old enough to go inside, I went to Cream Ridge. It was one of the first wineries I ever entered. And Tom Amabile was one of the nicest men I ever met. His gray-to-white hair was very neatly combed, and he was smartly dressed, with wire-rimmed glasses and a plaid madras shirt. He told me how he made wine. He showed me his tanks and other equipment. He told me how the process works. He answered all the questions a young novice might ask. He never hesitated. He loved to talk about wine and gave of himself freely. I never told him what my plans were. He never asked, though I think he probably knew more about me than I could guess about him. Such is the disadvantage of youth and the wisdom of age.

To me, it was like being invited into the Wonka factory. I felt like Charlie, marveling at the machinery, the tanks, the cases of empty bottles, and thousands of rolls of labels. Everywhere I looked, something else caught my attention. To me, for some reason I cannot even explain today, it was as exciting as being on a Hollywood back lot or behind the curtain in *The Wizard of Oz*.

Tom was a pioneer. Back then there were only a dozen or so wineries in the state. And New Jersey wines were scoffed at in those days. A self-taught winemaker, Tom began making wine for friends and family as a hobby and ultimately founded Cream Ridge Winery in 1988 with his wife, Joan, making fruit wines that received numerous medals as well as the 2005 Governor's Cup—the highest award in the state. Cream Ridge Winery was named New Jersey's first "Winery of the Year." He loved teaching the winemaking process and did so at Middlesex Community College.

I had not seen Tom in years. I had been to the winery countless times and he had answered every question I put to him, all with a smile on his face, waving his hand to invite me inside. And I was not the only one. He befriended dozens over the years, and he was just as generous with them. That was Tom. He had no luck growing grapes, but he could make other fruits shine as wine. His Cream Ridge Cherry Ciliegia Amabile was a revelation at the time.

My memories of this very, very generous man are as clear as ever. And I am ever grateful, humbled. The world has lost a very valuable man. He was one of the people whose shoulders the East Coast winemaking community stands on today. But most importantly for me, he was Willy Wonka. And I was hooked. Someday, I, too, would own a winery and make wine. And that's how it all started for me.

INTRODUCTION

I have been writing about wine for twenty years and editing and publishing books on wine, beer, and spirits for longer than that. I have worked with *Wine Spectator* and *The New York Times* on wine and cocktail books, as well as with Kevin Zraly from *Windows on the World Complete Wine Course*, wine columnist Matt Kramer, British TV wine celebrity Oz Clarke, sparkling wine expert Tom Stevenson, and the World Wine Guys. At tastings, I've met Francis Ford Coppola, Beau Barrett, George Tabor, Marvin Shanken, Jorge Muga Palacin, and numerous other folks.

So moved was I by wine that I bought a farm that had lain fallow for more than thirty years. With the help of my former wife, Dominique, we not only put the farm back on the agricultural map, but we created award-winning estate-grown wines that *Wine Enthusiast* rated 90 points or more. We cofounded the Hudson Berkshire Beverage Trail and the Hudson Berkshire Wine & Food Festival, which now attracts thousands of attendees every year. Throughout our time there, I helped to promote the wine industry on the East Coast and around the world.

Dominique and I separated and sold the winery in May 2020, three months after COVID had descended upon the world. Screw it, I thought. I bought myself a silver 2014 Mustang convertible with black leather interior (which everyone called my midlife crisis car, though I bought it to replace my previous convertible—whatever). I was determined to take a trip I had long wanted to make—drive across the country, and then up the Pacific Coast Highway, visiting as many wineries as I could.

I would not only stop in California, Oregon, and Washington, but in Pennsylvania, Ohio, New Jersey, Maryland, Virginia, and throughout New England. I didn't want to just visit the West Coast, I wanted to discover the wines all around America.

The media, funny enough, picked up on my trip. Driving across the country, drinking wine while the entire world was locked in their homes, apparently was noteworthy. Dave McIntyre wrote about my trip in an article entitled "Good Wine Is Now Being Made in Most Parts of the Country. Here's How to Find It" for *The Washington Post*.

"This year, of course, we're more or less stuck wherever 'here' happens to be, our wanderlust curtailed by the coronavirus pandemic. We can't all be like Carlo DeVito, who over the summer sold his Hudson-Chatham winery in New York's Hudson River Valley and set out on a cross-country wine adventure. We can follow along—DeVito chronicled his exploits as 'The Great American Winery Stroopwaffle' on his YouTube channel and his blog."

The article appeared in a half dozen newspapers that Dave's articles normally get picked up in. The Albany *Times-Union* also wrote about my vacation. "Carlo DeVito left his life behind this spring and partook in his own personal Rumspringa. Except, he had trouble remembering that term—Rumspringa—for when a young Amish person departs their known world and ventures into modernity in order to discover if they love and want to return to their rural, antiquated roots or remain part of contemporary culture," wrote Deanna Fox. "He called his adventure the Great American Winery Stroopwaffle."

I honestly couldn't remember the term "Rumspringa" at the time. And Babe Hack, someone very close to me, couldn't remember it either and offered up the word "Stroopwaffle" instead. We both laughed hysterically—but it stuck.

"Part self-discovery, part *Cannonball Run*, the goal was to visit 100 wineries across America and record his process in a series of YouTube videos and blog posts to help rekindle his love of wine and help others learn about the possibilities in little known winemaking regions," wrote Fox.

"DeVito wanted his trip to be more than a personal act of hedonism," wrote Fox. "He wanted this journey to be a shared experience…a chance to educate on how a pandemic and climate change have affected American winemaking and what the future may hold for the practice."

That summer I drove almost ten thousand miles, and visited more than a hundred wineries and distilleries around the country. My goal was not to go to the big places. I had already been to places like Robert Mondavi (whose tour is one of the best educational experiences in American wine). I wanted to visit wineries like mine. Boutique wineries. Farm wineries. I wanted to visit with the owner/winemakers around the country. Small artisanal producers like Schermeister, Madrigal, St. Clair Brown, Ehlers Estate, and William Harrison. We chatted, mostly outside at safe distances, talking farming, politics, and winemaking as we tasted various wines.

One of the most memorable things I have ever heard was something Kevin Zraly said in an interview. He had asked a well-known winemaker what the biggest difference was between winemaking now and winemaking twenty years ago. His winemaker friend said that was easy—communication. Back in the day, the Bordelais and the Burgundians did not like one another, dismissed one another, and certainly did not share farming secrets with their winemaking brethren. This was true of many of the classic winemaking regions. But since the 1990s, winemakers have come together as a community, regionally and worldwide.

When you own a vineyard or a winery, you're a farmer. And when you're a farmer, something is always going awry. A piece of equipment breaks down, or you run out of yeast, or you need corks, or a few extra cases of bottles. Something. Farmers help one another. And in this new day and age, not only do winemakers help one another, they talk. They talk crops. They talk harvest. They talk winemaking. Because they realize that, if their neighbor makes better wine, it will affect them. This was a clarion call of Robert Mondavi in the late 1960s and early 1970s. A rising tide lifts all boats. It ended up working in Napa and Sonoma. And it has continued to work across the United States.

I wound my way through Oregon and Washington, making sure I hit the wine trails and the quality producers in those states, stopping to taste and learn. I came back through Ohio, Western Pennsylvania, Western New York, and the Finger Lakes. I went down to Tennessee, Virginia, and New Jersey, and then back up for a swing through New England.

What I learned was this: while I love the wines of California, Oregon, and Washington, there is great wine being made all across the country, in every state of our union.

I tasted a fantastic Pinot Noir in Ohio. A mouthwatering Vinho Verde in Pennsylvania. Terrific Albariño in New Jersey, and memorable Viognier and Petit Manseng in Virginia. Wonderful, sophisticated fruit wines from Maine that would shock you. I found dozens of terrific Pétillant Naturels from around the country. Palatable Piquettes! There were whole-cluster co-ferments and natural wines. And loads of good red wines, from light bodied to big, chewy ones that made me close my eyes and smile. Is this heaven? No, it's the North Fork.

The farmers/winemakers I met along the way were extremely forthcoming. In even the most casual conversations, they shared their notes, the yeasts they were using, soaking times, and temperatures. They talked barrels and steel tanks, pumps, everything. No one put anyone down. Everyone was open to sharing and learning.

When someone asks me about wine and how they can learn about it, I shake my head. Such a big topic. The best book on the subject is *Windows on the World Complete Wine Course* by Kevin Zraly. He is absolutely the best teacher. You read it not as a book, but as a book within a book (each chapter is worth a week or two in an intensive course). *Wine for Dummies* by Ed McCarthy and Mary Ewing-Mulligan is also very good. And there are dozens of others.

But what there isn't, what doesn't exist, is a book explaining all the experimentation, all the small states, all the small regions, all the small movements that are going on in wine. And what there really isn't is a book that recommends bottles from small artisanal winemakers and explains what they are up to.

In the big picture, there are more wineries than ever before. According to the Wines Vines Analytics Winery Database, as of 2023 there were 11,691 wineries in the United States alone. Approximately 4,700 wineries were in California, 1,000 more in Washington and Oregon each, leaving more than 4,800 wineries across the rest of the country. Roughly 41.5 percent of all the wineries reside outside the West Coast. That's a lot of new wineries to try, and a lot of very, very cool little movements going on in the industry.

That's what this book is. We're going to cover American wine—from all over the country, since great wine is being made everywhere. There are classic versions of all your favorite wines—as well as new grapes, experimental wines, reinvented styles, and cutting-edge winemaking techniques.

My trip was about exploration. And this book is about enjoying that exploration. The wine world is not the same as it was twenty years ago, with just a dozen wine regions. It's gotten more complex, and I think it's gotten that much more interesting. This is a course in wine—on the cutting edge.

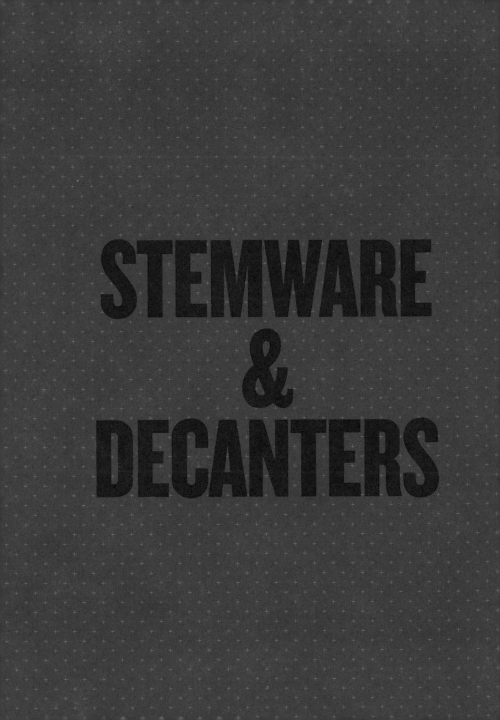

STEMWARE & DECANTERS

Stemware is as important to wine tasting as the wine itself. The right stemware can accentuate the wine and help the liquid reach its full potential. Can't you drink it out of a Solo cup? Sure. You could also eat caviar or foie gras off a paper plate, but it's not going to yield the optimal experience. Having owned a farm for a decade and a half, believe me, we learned to keep most everything as simple as possible (especially with two boys)—but there are certain things that make life better.

THE ONLY WINEGLASSES YOU WILL EVER NEED

People ask me all the time: "Does a wineglass make a difference?" And here is the story I always tell in response. My then wife, Dominique, and I were in the fourth year of owning Hudson-Chatham Winery. We had agreed to join our friends Mike and Jill at a charming little Italian restaurant in Hudson, New York, called Vico (it's since closed). The owners, Mark and Adam, were friends of ours. We'd been among their first customers.

We had brought a bottle of our Baco Noir Reserve, which was then being served in Il Bucco and Rouge Tomate in New York City. We were happy to pay the corkage fee, and eager to share the wine with our friends. I handed the bottle to the waitress, who promptly took it away for opening. She shortly returned with four large Riedel Burgundy/Pinot Noir–styled glasses with a decent pour in each glass. We felt so decadent and ritzy drinking the wine in this way. At our country home at the vineyard, even in the tasting room, we had used lesser glasses for costs' sake, trying to keep our little family endeavor on a budget.

We were all so impressed. We clinked glasses and offered some casual toasts. This was our first time drinking our own wine from such glasses.

They seemed innately reserved, by some strange, immutable law, for "good" wines. "Real" wines. But certainly not ours.

Then we brought the glasses to our lips. The aromas were intoxicating. Big notes of blueberry, raspberry, brambleberry, and cranberry. A certain earthiness. Lovely tannins and a long, delicious finish filled with fruit and spice. Despite our companions' pleased faces, I immediately drew a curious face, and called our server over. Dominique, too, was unsure.

"What can I get you?"

"I think there has been some mistake," I told her. "I wanted our wine. I think you poured someone else's wine for us by accident?" She looked like she was being punked.

"No," she said. "That's the wine you brought."

"It is?" I asked. "Are you sure?"

"Yes, here it is," and she stepped away two feet, and showed us the bottle. "If you don't like it, we can get you something else. We won't charge you the corkage."

Dominique and I were both gobsmacked. We were both thinking, "This is our wine?" I had drunk our wines from barrels and tanks, in little Glencairn glasses, port glasses, jelly jars. But never in a real wineglass. That's the difference the right stemware can make.

Riedel (established in 1756) and Spiegelau (founded in 1521) are two of the most well-known of the wine stemware manufacturers in the world. When they came out with their first lines of specialized wineglasses, I wanted to collect them all. I was the worst of the worst. I wanted the large Bordeaux white and red glasses, the Burgundy/Pinot Noir glasses, the Chardonnay and the Riesling, and, of course, the port glasses as well. I would sacrifice all the others, but those were "must-haves." As the years wore on, I stopped using half of my stemware. I didn't like washing all those glasses (that I paired with each appropriate wine), and, in truth, a few sufficed for the many, without the degradation of taste.

What follows is the glassware I stuck with.

Coupe and Flute

I love both of these glasses for sparkling wine, but there are remarkable differences between the two. If you're single and living in a small apartment, the coupe might be better for you. Simply put, it never looks bad with sparkling wine in it and, as long as you are not filling it to the brim, you'll finish it off quickly enough to have another without the wine going flat.

Another strong selling point of the coupe is that it has multiple uses. It's the perfect and preferred glass for many cocktails, including a Manhattan, Gimlet, Boulevardier, and a number of others. It will be among the most used of your barware.

For those who want to intensify the bubbles, a classic flute is best. Long, elegant strands of tiny bubbles linger in the glass like miniature strings of pearls. The flute intensifies the aromas and bubbles of a sparkling wine, making for a better tasting experience. And a terribly elegant one as well.

Bordeaux Glass

Bordeaux or Grand Vin Bordeaux wineglasses are tulip shaped and generally hold about 22 ounces of wine. That does not mean you fill them even halfway, as that's a lot of wine. The idea of the glass is to aerate the wine, to incorporate air into it so that the wine opens up more. I prefer the bigger ones, which I use for both red and white.

Burgundy Glass

I consider the Grand Burgundy/Pinot Noir–style glasses the best tasting glasses of all. The bulb on a Burgundy/Pinot Noir glass is wider at the base, thus, there is more wine-to-oxygen exposure, meaning the wine has more room to breathe. Also, the top of the glass is funneled more acutely than in a Bordeaux glass, so the aroma is directed upward more intensely. This type of glass works just as well for whites as it does for reds.

Port Wineglass

You do not use a large glass for port, sherry, or ice wines. Generally speaking, I like the Libby 8551 Tasting Glass. It looks like the Grand Vin Bordeaux glass, but in miniature. It has a short stem and a capacity of 10½ ounces. It is perfect for small pours of intense wines, allowing for aeration as well as a focusing of the nose like the larger glasses. Durable and quite versatile.

BREATHING AND DECANTING

Breathing/decanting is a controversial subject. Some absolutely insist on it. Others shrug, saying today's wines are made to be ready to drink straight from the bottle. According to famed wine expert, friend, and author Matt Kramer, traditionally there were two reasons aficionados decanted. First, there usually was sediment in wine, especially red wine. Also, wines were "less than perfectly made." Decanting allowed unattractive odors to blow off, reinforcing the idea that aeration improved

COUPE

BORDEAUX

PORT

BURGUNDY

FLUTE

wines. According to Kramer, decanting was, at a particular point in the history of winemaking, a practical issue.

Breathing means simply that you open the bottle and let the wine sit for some period of time in the bottle before serving it. Could be an hour, several hours—in the way-back times, it might have been several days.

Decanting is the practice of removing the wine from the bottle, leaving the sediment behind and allowing for extra aeration.

To Decant or Not to Decant?

The answer is, it depends. The large glasses we use today often perform the aeration that decanting used to offer.

Also, older wines tend to fall apart faster if decanted. Having worked with and spoken with numerous wine experts, the experience is that older wines (ten or more years old) quickly deteriorate once exposed to air. This is especially the case with older Pinot Noirs and lighter reds. I have heard multiple stories, and experienced it once myself, of lighter reds falling apart before the second half of a decanted older bottle was finished. Generally speaking, Sangiovese, Chianti Classico, and Chianti Riserva do not require decanting.

Conversely, younger wines can benefit from air. But this can be accomplished by aggressively swirling the wine around in your glass—swirl, reverse the swirl, and then double back to make sure the agitation is complete. I might repeat this a second or even a third time, depending on how big the wine is.

"A good rule to follow: Do as the Romans do—or in this case, the French. For example, in Burgundy, they never decant their Beaujolais or other delicate wines," advises Kevin Zraly. According to him, only a big Cabernet Sauvignon, a Merlot, or a big Zinfandel will benefit from such exposure.

But there is this to consider. "Using a decanter eliminates what might be called 'label hypnosis.' Too many wine lovers have the deer-in-the-headlights syndrome," wrote Matt Kramer in *Wine Spectator*. "They are transfixed by the sight of the label. They can't take their eyes—and their palates—off it."

I tend to decant no more than an hour before serving. Kramer likes fifteen minutes.

Decanters

I will not lie. I have several pairs of beautiful crystal wine decanters, the most exquisite dust catchers I have ever owned. Stunning. Impressive. Old-world. I never use them.

The best wine decanter is one based on the old ship captain's decanter, with an ultrawide base. Why? Because one bottle poured into this decanter will experience the largest wine-to-air ratio possible, allowing for maximum aeration. These do not need to be expensive. The Better Homes & Gardens Glass Wine Decanter, Bella Vino Premium Crystal Glass Tannin Softening 1,200 ml Elegant Wine Decanter (both available from Walmart), or the Koios Wine Decanter (available on Amazon) are all $20 and under and work beautifully. Can you buy more elegant ones? Absolutely! But I like the performance and the durability that these wine decanters offer.

When decanting a big red wine, you might want to buy an aerator or a funnel with a microscreen to trap any sediment and prevent it from going into the decanter, especially if you like wines from small artisanal houses.

A final note: Decanters are difficult to clean. They don't work in the dishwasher. My best advice is to clean them before you go to bed and set them upside down to dry. If you let them sit, the wine dries on the bottom and is hard to remove. One needs to stay vigilant.

TASTING WINE

The first thing you need to remember about wine is that it is food. Yes, it is an essential part of a quality dining experience; whether you are drinking a high-end wine, like a first-growth Bordeaux, or a jug wine from California, or a Three Buck Chuck (Charles Shaw) from Trader Joe's, wine adds a new and impressive dimension to any meal. But that is not what I mean. To appreciate wine, we must experience it as food.

THE TASTING EXPERIENCE

The classic steps to tasting include see, swirl, smell, sip, and savor. That has not changed. Each step is important in understanding and appreciating your wine. If you're tasting, you're committing to experiencing the wine in a much more in-depth manner. It's an education. Otherwise, you're just drinking. Nothing wrong with that. But when you're tasting, it's about understanding the wine.

As a writer, I'm always curious about the story behind a wine, the winery, and the winemaker. Is this something that's quaffable? Is this something a little more special—a reserve, for example? Is this a new grape or an experimental wine? Is it a blend? Was it traditionally fermented or something different? Oaked or unoaked?

That said, I reserve the ritual of tasting a wine for only the first time I experience it. After that, I simply drink it with friends and family. Tasting wine is about learning; drinking wine with family and friends is about experiencing the wine.

SEE

Why do we look at wine? Any time you eat a burger, a steak, a lobster, you look at it, right? Isn't that key to a dining experience? When you are in a restaurant and the waiter sets down a dish at a neighboring table, I bet you've asked, "Hey, what is that?" How about when you watch your favorite food show on television and you start getting hungry?

In the case of wine, you are looking for color and clarity. They tell you a lot about a wine. Let's start with color. Usually, a deeper color indicates a bigger wine. A deep gold or a deep purple typically means you're in for a bigger, heavier wine. A lighter color tends to suggest that the wine is lighter in body.

Clarity is also of some importance. Unless you're drinking a natural-styled wine (which can be as cloudy as ale), clarity is usually an indicator that the wine is fully matured and that fermentation is complete. You should generally be able to "read" through a light- or medium-bodied wine; this means that, if you lean your glass over a page of text, you should be able to read the text. Bigger wines, like Cabernet Sauvignon and Zinfandel, can sometimes be opaque. This indicates a chewy, powerful wine, one you will bite into.

SWIRL

To taste wine, you only pour a small amount into your glass. You'll want to mix the wine with air by swirling it. Stemware is appropriately shaped and sized to enable air to mix with the wine and help accentuate the wine's scent, not to drink a large bowlful. One finger width of wine (sideways, the thickness of your finger!) is all you need to taste.

When you swirl, it's a gentle swirl, not an Olympic event. The best way to learn to swirl is to leave the glass on the table when you do it, gently rotating the base of the glass in a small circular motion. The wine will swirl easily—two or three times usually is sufficient. The idea is to coat the inside of the glass with the wine. This does two things: first, it aerates the wine. Adding oxygen to wine (or letting it "breathe") allows it to fully develop its nose by enhancing the wine's inherent aromas. Swirling also allows you to evaluate the wine's viscosity or thickness. When the wine settles back down into the bowl of the glass, the inside of the glass will be coated with rivulets of wine, known as "legs." Pronounced legs that thickly coat the inside of the glass and take a long time to drip back into the bowl indicate greater viscosity; the greater the viscosity, the bigger and chewier the wine. Legs are also a sign of the wine's sugar and alcohol content—the more pronounced the legs are, the higher these two elements will generally be.

SMELL

Ever walk into a home where a chicken has been roasting or someone is making a big pot of tomato sauce or baking a pie? As with every food experience, smell is an important part of tasting wine.

The wineglasses of today intensify the sensation of smell. By swirling the wine, you are spiraling its aromas up near the rim of the glass. What are we hoping to find when we smell? Good and bad things. For example, things like apple, pear, and tropical fruits in white wines are good smells. Cherry, raspberry, plum, and other red fruits are excellent smells to be found in red wines. However, mushroom, dank basement, and vinegar are not good smells in either whites or reds and can indicate a wine gone bad.

In wine tasting, the word "aroma" is generally used for those smells that best identify with the grape type, e.g., lychee with Gewürztraminer and blackberry or cassis with Cabernet Sauvignon grapes. "Bouquet" usually identifies smells that come from the finished, aged wine. Sometimes these smells are the result of the winemaking process or fermentation, while other notes might come from aging in barrels. Apricot and/or honey can be found in intense dessert wines like Sauternes or ice wines, a result of the juice's concentration during winemaking. Tobacco and/or spices are often associated with Cabernet Sauvignon, deriving from the wine's extended contact with the grape skins. Wine professionals tend to choose smells and flavors that the average person can identify with.

SIP

When I say sip, I mean sip. Not gulp. The idea is to really try to taste the wine. Foremost, you are tasting for fruit, and also acidity and tannin, which are natural components of wine and can enhance flavor.

A decent amount of acidity helps keep the fruit taste fresh and alive.

After the first sip, you should wait 40 to 60 seconds and evaluate. Are you still tasting the fruit? The amount of time it lasts tells you a lot about a wine—the longer lasting the fruit, the better the wine.

Tannin is a big component of wine, especially red wine. It is experienced as a dryness in the mouth at the mid and back palate after taking a sip.

Hold a Hand Over the Top of Your Glass

This is a tip from Kevin Zraly, America's first great wine instructor (and cellar master), for best capturing the essence of a wine's bouquet, or aroma. While swirling the wine, hold one hand over the top of the glass, sealing it lightly, to trap the aroma of the wine. When you are done swirling, bring the glass to your nose, then lift your hand up to release concentrated scents from the glass. Try it. It makes a huge difference.

The sensation is very much akin to drinking tea without cream, milk, or sugar. Tannins are present in grape skins (particularly in red grape varieties), and can also be transferred to wines through oak barrels during aging.

SAVOR

How is savor different from sip? Sip gives you the initial taste response to the wine, like that first bite of a steak or lick of an ice cream cone. To savor, however, is completely different. To do it properly, hold the wine in your mouth a good 15 to 30 seconds to let the wine penetrate your taste buds. This is why you see a lot of wine professionals swish a sip around their mouths. Then you want to stop, and for the next 30 seconds or so, try to decipher what you are tasting. Acidity comes from the sides of your mouth. Sweetness on the tip of your tongue. Tannins at the back of your tongue.

Once you have had a chance to savor the wine, let's further evaluate it. First, is it balanced? Balance means exactly what it says. If a wine is too sweet, with no acidity, most winemakers would say it is out of balance. If the wine is too tannic at the end and there is no lingering fruit, again, the wine is considered out of balance.

A wine should start off with fruit, both on the nose and on the palate. While a long list of other flavors and sensations might come into play, at the end of your taste, about 15 to 30 seconds or so after you have swallowed, you should still have a lingering flavor of fruit.

The best wines will leave a lovely fruit flavor in your mouth that, in the best instances, can linger as long as 60 seconds. A good Pinot Noir will leave behind the essence of cherry for a long time. A good Albariño or Sauvignon Blanc will leave a lingering citrus flavor. Dessert wines bring apricot, pineapple, and honey notes that linger.

Now consider the wine's complexity. This usually refers to the connections the taster may draw from their sip. There should be layers. How many different fruits can you smell or taste? Are there spices? Is there a hint of wood? With older wines, maybe some dryness or a hint of fallen leaves? Is there an earthiness? A hint of cocoa or mocha? Is there a dash of pepper? And how do all these flavors mingle? Is the wine presenting only one note? Or are there flavors shifting from one end of the wine to another? Are they blending nicely, or is it a big plop?

Like a good burger or a great roast chicken, there are flavors that are pleasing, that follow one from another. Aromas. Salt. Spice. Fire. A wine is just the same. There must be a pleasing line that runs through it, to keep you coming back for more.

When you're reading notes on a wine, it's important to be able to understand what the taster is trying to communicate. When a writer says a wine has "notes of," it means these are the strongest flavors one can identify in the wine that can be used as descriptors. "Hints" or "whiffs" are the secondary notes. They are lighter, and may not linger as long or as prominently, but they are there. In a Pinot Noir, you're likely to get a strong cherry note up front, but in the background there are other flavors, perhaps violets, or blueberries, or vanilla? This is what wine descriptions are based on, so that a consumer can better understand what they are buying and looking for in the wine.

Flavors to Savor

There are whole books dedicated to the vocabulary of wine description, actual dictionaries. According to wine expert Bernard Klem, there are more than 36,000 descriptors. Here are some common words used to describe wine, both its aromas and its flavors.

White Wine

Citrus: lemon, lime, grapefruit

Stone fruit: apple, pear, peach, apricot, fig

Tropical fruit: melon, pineapple, banana

Floral notes: orange blossom, honeysuckle

Herbal: grass or grassiness

Vegetal: green pepper

Spice: clove, allspice, nutmeg

Oak: vanilla, oak

Smoke: smoke, toast, burnt toast, charred

Buttery: honey, caramel, butterscotch

Red Wine

Berry: strawberry, raspberry, blackberry, cassis

Stone fruit: cherry, plum

Dried fruits: jam, raisin, prune

Floral notes: violet, rose petal

Chocolate: cocoa, dark chocolate, mocha

Earthiness: bacon, leather, barnyard, fallen leaves

Herbal: grass or grassiness

Vegetal: green pepper

Spice: pepper, cinnamon, clove

Oak: vanilla, oak

Smoke: smoke, toast, burnt toast, charred

Faults

Faults in wine announce themselves in classic ways: the wine can smell like sulfur (rotten eggs), nail polish, mushrooms, or a moldy basement. It might have a lot of acid or might taste too much like vinegar. A white wine might have a lot of crystals that have settled at the bottom of the bottle. It might smell like chicken manure. These are all indications that something has gone wrong during the winemaking process.

Sending a wine back at a restaurant because it has faults like these is perfectly acceptable. Your sommelier, cellar master, or server should be able to confirm them. On the other hand, you can't send back a perfectly good glass or bottle of wine because you thought it would be something else; that is rude and, worst of all, stupid.

A NOTE ON VERTICAL TASTINGS

What is a vertical tasting? It's when you taste the same wine over a series of vintages. Assembling a classic string of vintages of a Pinot Noir from Oregon, or Cabernet Sauvignon from California, or Merlot from Long Island, or Riesling from the Finger Lakes with a group of friends can be affordable and fun (especially if everyone chips in). It can easily be done with international wines as well.

It's sometimes easier to choose more affordably priced wines, which are plentiful, and easier to find. Just buy the same label over five or six different years. See if you can score one older bottle, and then have fun—it's an amazing learning experience that you can share with friends. If you're already a collector, take that vertical you've been saving, put together a guest list of your friends, and enjoy!

Kevin Zraly was the first person to truly open my eyes to vertical tastings. Later in my career, I was lucky enough to host a vertical tasting of a decade's worth of my own wines. A great thrill. It doesn't always have to be a fancy event. Back in 2020, I sat with celebrated New England wine expert Todd Trzaskos and winemaker Chris Granstrom (who founded Lincoln Peak Vineyard in New Haven, Vermont) up in Vermont. Todd and I had dropped by to say hello to Chris, who opened up for us his most recent vintage of Marquette. After some discussion, he opened up another and another—until, finally, we'd opened quite a few bottles of the wine. By the end, we'd tasted a 2008, a 2010, and a 2018, among others. Todd and I were astounded. I think, looking back, that even Chris was surprised. The Marquettes, all of which were exceptional, had aged well. They continued to show great fruit, even the 2008 wine. They showed that they had staying power and had melded together perfectly. The fruit had mellowed, but not to the point of disappearing. That's the fun of it, learning about the wine and how wine ages.

In Kevin's master classes, he always tastes the wines youngest to oldest. He admonishes everyone to take only a small sip of the first and youngest wine, to leave as much as possible in the glass. In the tasting I participated in, among the youngest vintages there were only shades of difference. However, around the seven- to eight-year mark, the fruit began to be more muted, more of a stew rather than identifiable individual fruits. And their finishes were silkier. By the ten-year mark, the fruit was still there, but again, somewhat indecipherable to me. But there were also the classic notes of spice, herbs, and the slightest hints of fallen leaves and tomato.

After tasting the oldest wine, Kevin instructed us to go back and taste that first wine again. I was astonished! My wineglass smelled like someone had coated the inside of it with Mrs. Butterworth's or Log Cabin. It smelled like a maple lollipop. It tasted sweet. And my first thought was, "Who the hell put something in my wine?"

Kevin explained that the difference between the new wine and the older wines was that the components in the wine had not yet coalesced. While the older wines had integrated, the new wine was still very much a wine of parts. The older wines, while still exhibiting great character, had melded into something else. All were excellent, but it showed the effects of cellaring and how wine ages. It is a tremendous learning tool, and I hope you experience it one day.

FERMENTATION

"**W**ine is a living thing." I roll my eyes every time I hear that. But it is absolutely true. Annoying, but true. It's not so much that the wine is alive as it is that the yeast used to make the wine is. Put simply, as I used to tell folks on our winery tours, yeasts are like college students. They eat sugar all day long, they fart, and copious amounts of alcohol are involved. In the case of wine, yeasts are added to juice, where they consume the sugar. The result is that they turn that sugar into alcohol, while at the same time expelling a tremendous amount of CO_2. Yeasts only quit when there's no more sugar left, and/or when the percentage of alcohol has gotten high enough to knock them out—again, just like college students. This process is called fermentation.

For anyone who has worked with yeast, you know there are stories to tell. My most memorable was when I was preparing to make a large batch of Pinot Grigio. I got a five-gallon bucket of warm water and some sugar. I poured in the correct amount of yeast and whipped it up into a well-aerated slurry. I like to give the yeast time to develop a nice frothy head (like on a pint of Guinness) before adding it to the juice—that way you know it's working before you pour it into the fermenter with the pressed juice. So, I let it rest to give it time to get going.

I was then called away for about twenty minutes. What greeted me when I returned was something out of *Ghostbusters*. The bucket was belching up a muddy column of yeasty lava, which was now all over the counters and moving across the floor with seeming intent. It just kept coming. It took us an hour to clean up (using beer pitchers, a snow shovel, and dustpans) and another half hour to make another batch. It was the ultimate proof that yeasts are alive.

Today, there are three primary ways yeasts are used in modern wine-making. Some winemakers like to inoculate their juice with specially designed yeast; this comprises the large bulk of the commercial wine-making world. Others make a slurry from indigenous materials local to their farm to make a yeast that will contribute to the final wine's sense of place or terroir. The third, which is known as the open-top method (used mostly by natural winemakers), allows airborne yeast to do the job. All of these have their uses and help position and shape the wine we drink. There's no one "right" way to do it. It's a matter of personal taste. Three chefs may make an omelet but could get there using three different methods. Winemaking is much the same.

CLASSIC WINE YEAST INOCULATION

Wine yeasts were isolated by famed French scientist Louis Pasteur; his groundbreaking research was the backbone of the winemaking industry for more than a hundred years.

"Pasteur was the first to demonstrate experimentally that fermented beverages result from the action of living yeast transforming glucose into ethanol," wrote L. Alba-Lois, PhD, and C. Segal-Kischinevzky, MSc, in *Nature Education* in 2010. "Moreover, Pasteur demonstrated that only microorganisms are capable of converting sugars into alcohol from grape juice, and that the process occurs in the absence of oxygen. He concluded that fermentation is a vital process, and he defined it as res-piration without air."

Never before has yeast played as important a part in the winemaking process as it does today. These days, a winemaker literally has hun-dreds of different strains of yeast to choose from. Prepared or cultured yeasts (as they are known) are sold through laboratories and industrial concerns. Many of these have been isolated in labs or created by mixing different strains. A vintner can find a yeast that promotes fruit flavors, or one that isolates red fruit flavors while stifling acidity. Another might be aimed at whites, to promote the fruit as well as floral notes in the nose. You can find yeasts that have been isolated from French or Italian strains if your goal is to achieve a result closer to an Italian or French ideal.

This is a long way from twenty or thirty years ago, when there were about five manufacturers (like Red Star and Lalvin) and maybe fifty yeasts to choose from. Today producers (including Scott Laboratories, Vintner's Harvest, White Labs, and Wyeast Laboratories) offer inventive cultured yeasts that can encourage flavors or help mitigate possible faults. In general, these yeasts allow winemakers to exert a lot more control in the cellar and maintain a consistent flavor profile across their products and numerous vintages. It is a brave new world.

Sometimes, as a winemaker, you find the one yeast that works really well with your fruit. And life is simple. A magic bullet, as it were. Other winemakers may mix several yeasts because they are hoping to hit a number of notes, which using only one yeast might not satisfy. This is where the controversy takes place. One side says that, in the long run, the dominant yeast will take over. The other side says, possibly, but by that time, some of the lesser yeasts will have had some impact on the final product. Again, different chefs, different omelets.

Most commonly, the yeasts are added once the juice has been crushed or pressed, depending on the process the winemaker is using (whites tend to be pressed, reds crushed, though there are exceptions on both accounts). The yeasts are sprinkled on top so that they can access both the oxygen they need and the sugar in the juice.

WILD YEAST

"Indigenous, spontaneous, natural, aboriginal, feral, native, endemic, ambient or wild—no matter what you want to call it, the art of making wine without adding commercial yeast is gaining favor in the U.S.," wrote Richard Olsen-Harbich. "Today, many of the world's finest wines are still produced with native yeasts. These winemakers see indigenous yeasts as integral to the authenticity of their wines and feel that natural fermentation imparts a distinct regional character."

Formerly the head winemaker at Bedell Cellars, Rich wrote the American Viticultural Area (AVA) description for Long Island back in the 1980s, and started the certified sustainable movement on the North Fork. He has long been a fan of indigenous yeast fermentation. "Every year we ask everyone on Bedell's staff to find something native to bring in and add to the culture. Items include flowers, seashells, rocks, soil, and water from our surrounding beaches," Rich told pioneering Long Island winemaker Louisa Hargrave. "We even have a local native arrowhead that we use in the starter every year. It's both fun and very spiritual and our culture truly becomes something even more than just an indigenous fermentation. It becomes something of the essence of the North Fork and it's something that is in every wine we make.

"The overriding trait to me is a saline minerality which is a subtle and beautiful attribute in most all of our wines," he told Hargrave. "Our terroir gives us everything we need. The result is wines that are moderate in alcohol with crisp acidity and great balance. This is what we do best and what so many other New World regions are desperately trying to achieve right now. For me, it is foremost and essential in the quest to define terroir, because it is just so—a product of its own environment. In essence, terroir begets terroir."

Two of my favorites from Bedell Cellars are their Sauvignon Blanc and Cabernet Franc. The Sauvignon Blanc is made from pressing whole clusters of sustainably farmed estate-grown fruit. It is fermented with indigenous yeasts. The resulting wine remains in stainless steel. This is truly a mouthwatering wine. "Many on the East Coast make fruity Sauvignon with grass and green notes," wrote Mark Squires of the *Wine Advocate*. "What they sometimes lack, however, is some zing and zest—I love the way Bedell's Sauvignons accomplish that."

The Cabernet Franc is made from hand-selected, sustainably farmed estate grapes. The crushed fruit is fermented with indigenous yeasts. After pressing, the wine is aged in neutral French oak barrels. The resulting wine is smooth and silky, with tons of fresh fruit. "Distinctly minerally on the nose with bright red fruits and subtle floral notes. Red fruits carry over to a supple-but-fresh palate with complex herbal and earthy flavors. A real cabernet franc lover's cabernet franc," wrote Lenn Thompson for *Press Fraction*.

OPEN-TOP FERMENTATION

On the other end of the country, general manager Craig Camp surveys his domain, Troon Vineyard, in Grants Pass, Oregon. Troon is regenerative, organic, and Demeter Biodynamic Certified for wine growing and farming. Demeter USA is the only certifier for biodynamic farms and products in America.

"At Troon Vineyard, everything we do is focused on supporting natural systems and getting out of their way. Our soils and plants are well suited to do their jobs. So are the native yeasts that populate our farm. These indigenous yeast populations are unique to our environment and are an essential component of what makes Troon, Troon," wrote Camp.

Troon's winemaker, Nate Wall, considers himself a minimalist, meaning he wants to stay as much out of nature's way as possible. "It starts with a pretty big philosophical divide, on the one hand, with the cultured yeast, where the winemaker has a lot of control, to assert a winemaking style onto a wine." Wall concedes that for some larger brands, consistency from vintage to vintage, and bottle to bottle, is extremely important. "There's a thumbprint on the winemaking style. People can get to know that style, and some people look for that style."

Introducing indigenous or native yeasts, the winemaker is embracing what Wall refers to as "this fundamentally chaotic and more complex natural system." This is sometimes referred to as spontaneous fermentation. "This allows for vintage variation, it allows for an expression of terroir. You end up ceding a large amount of control away from yourself as the winemaker, basically giving that control to this complex soup of microbes that are present in your wine," said Wall.

Open-top fermentation sounds almost exactly like what it is. The grapes are fermented in large bins. Winemakers leave the crushed fruit open to the air, hoping to build up a good-sized population of airborne yeasts, which also have the benefit of being free. Another selling point of open-top fermentation is that it generally keeps the heat slightly lower because it can escape. As red wine rests in these bins or fermenters, a cap develops as the crushed grape skins float to the top of the water column. This rise provides two benefits: it limits the air-to-wine ratio, and it collects still more yeast.

Commercial winemakers often keep their wines in controlled fermenters, where oxygen is limited and carefully controlled. But for open-top fermentations, the major moment comes when the winemaker decides to close the lid, and hopes that nature takes care of the rest. Overexposure to air can develop volatile acidity, giving the wine the taste of vinegar. But when it is done right, there is no better version of terroir, where the land, the weather, and the uniqueness of the local airborne yeasts combine to give the wine a real sense of place.

"When we've had genetic sequencing done on our ferments, many of the yeasts identified do not even have a name. That is very exciting. They are part of who we are as a winery and farm," wrote Camp.

I very much like a number of wines from Troon, including their Vermentino and Syrah. "They love to grow on this farm and in this mesoclimate," Camp said of the two varieties. "They are easy to farm and the chemistry is beautiful. They naturally produce the lower alcohol and higher acid we aspire to make, while still producing complex, full-flavored wines." Both are fermented in French oak barrels. The Vermentino has lovely floral notes followed by citrus zest and honeysuckle. Full-blown citrus comes across the palate, with apples, pears, and white peach. There is also a savory note to the wine. Delicious. Reggie Solomon of *Wine Casual* says this of the Syrah: "Deep-intensity purple in color, this wine has an aromatic, medium-plus-intensity nose of raspberry, dried blackberry, black plum and red cherry."

Yeast has become another instrument in the winemaker's tool kit. In the past, winemakers used different tools to change the flavor of their wines, from oak barrels to cement tanks to stainless steel. Some were fermented for short or long periods, whole cluster or crushed, or a blend. The growing role of yeast has made the new age of wine even more interesting.

THE BIG
TWELVE

Kevin Zraly, best-selling author of *Windows on the World Complete Wine Course*, says that there are only six grapes you need to know: Riesling, Sauvignon Blanc, and Chardonnay for whites and Pinot Noir, Merlot, and Cabernet Sauvignon for reds. By and large I believe he is correct, though I would add six more to expand your palate and experience—Pinot Grigio, Gewürztraminer, and Viognier for whites and Cabernet Franc, Syrah, and Zinfandel for reds.

It took some time before I understood the differences. At first I drank big, dry Cabernet Sauvignons with everything. From there, things opened up into a grand experiment.

The varietal that made the biggest impact on me was a California wine. We had gone to Napa and I was desperate to try Turley Old Vines Zinfandel. It was a cult wine at the time, hard to find. A unicorn. On the East Coast, even the most dialed-in wine collectors had a hard time securing a bottle.

We went to the Wappo Bar Bistro (which, sadly, no longer exists). The food was excellent. They had Turley on the menu. We ordered it immediately. The wine was incredible. Super concentrated, not just dark cherry and dark raspberry, but cassis and lekvar. It was a deep color and the flavors were massive.

On the following pages you'll find the Primary Six and then the Secondary Six white and red grapes every wine drinker should know.

2021 NAPA VALLEY ZINFANDEL TURLEY ESTATE TURLEY

Varietal Wines &
Frank Schoonmaker

Frank Schoonmaker is not a name most wine drinkers know, but he affected the wine world in a way few people have. A veteran of World War II, he was the author of several influential wine books and was a major promoter and importer of Burgundy wines. Beginning in the 1940s, it was Schoonmaker who insisted that American winemakers find a new vocabulary to sell American wine.

In Europe, the local viticultural organizations set requirements. Regions specialize in grapes. A label using the Burgundy name is required to be Pinot Noir or Chardonnay. Beaujolais has to be made from Gamay Noir. Red Bordeaux is limited to five grapes—Cabernet Sauvignon, Malbec, Merlot, Cabernet Franc, and Petit Verdot. Champagne is made from Chardonnay, Pinot Noir, and Pinot Meunier.

Schoonmaker knew that America's wine regions were still in their infancy, with no regulation as to what they were growing. Wines at that time were called "New York Champagne" or "California Bordeaux." He wanted the winemakers to forge their own identities, and advocated naming wines after the grape varieties that dominated in the bottle. This concept was finally embraced by winemakers in the late 1960s and through the 1970s. Today in the United States, to be called Cabernet Sauvignon, or Pinot Noir, or Chardonnay, a wine must be 75 percent that grape. As much as 25 percent might be something else, a long-held winemaking tradition, done to add more fruit, more tannin or backbone, more color, and/or acidity to a wine.

PRIMARY WHITES

Riesling

Riesling is made all around the world. It is best known in the Rhine region of Germany, where it was popularized. Today it is also made in France, Australia, New Zealand, and Austria, among other countries. In North America, the three largest growing regions for Riesling are the Finger Lakes in New York, Washington State, and Canada's Niagara region.

Many people know Riesling as a sweet wine only. I absolutely gravitated toward it when I was younger for that reason. But as I got older, I began to appreciate the drier versions and how well they pair with lighter fare. I also love the "petrol" note on really fine Rieslings, which is an acquired taste.

I love Canadian Riesling. Vineland Estates Winery Elevation St. Urban Riesling from the Niagara Escarpment is an explosion of lemon and lime zest and fresh-cut peaches. Sue-Ann Staff Estate Winery Robert's Block Riesling is made from the oldest block of Riesling on the estate, also in the Niagara region, and is named in honor of her great-great-great grandfather Robert Staff. Canvasback Royal Slope Riesling, made with grapes from the Lawrence and Frenchman Hills Vineyards in the Royal Slope region of Columbia Valley, exudes blood orange, pineapple, white peach, and candied ginger.

I have to give a shout-out to the Rieslings of New York, which I have promoted my entire career. If you want to know more about winemaking in the Finger Lakes, read Evan Dawson's *Summer in a Glass*. Chief among my favorites is Keuka Lake Vineyards Falling Man Vineyard Dry Riesling, with its big notes of tropical fruit and a nice dose of petrol fumes. I also love Anthony Road Wine Company's Riesling Dry; again, it presents all my favorite notes of Riesling—mouthwatering and super drinkable.

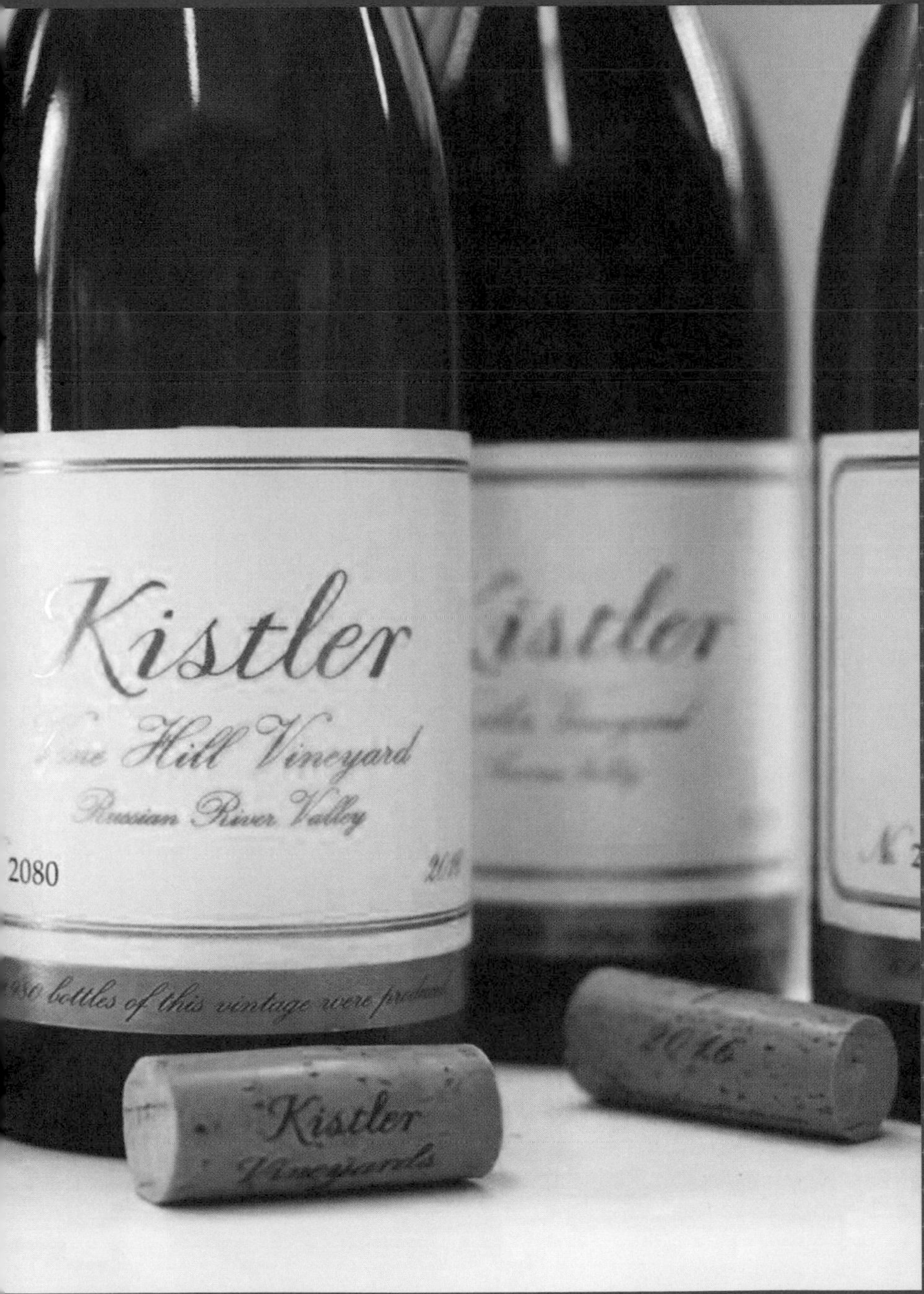
Kistler
Russian River Valley
2080
Kistler

Hermann J. Wiemer Vineyard HJW Vineyard Riesling is made from the fruit of vines planted in 1977. Big mineral notes with terrific acidity, this is an elegant, beautiful wine. It's a limited edition and hard to come by; their Riesling Dry is an excellent substitute. Ravines Wine Cellars Dry Riesling and Dry Riesling Argetsinger Vineyard are both super aromatic, with bursts of great citrus and lovely, lip-smacking acidity. The Rieslings from Buttonwood Grove Winery, Silver Thread Vineyard, New Vines Winery, Trestle Thirty One, and McGregor Vineyard are also recommended. Across the border in Connecticut, there's the dry and refreshingly fruity Stonington Vineyards Riesling.

My first Riesling love from Washington State was Eroica from Columbia Valley. It is a collaboration between famed Riesling producer Dr. Loosen Estate of Germany and Chateau Ste. Michelle Winery. Since 1999, the Eroica line has been a perennial favorite of wine writers everywhere, and with good reason. Another one of my favorites is Two Mountain Winery Riesling from Zillah. Terrific flavor, with a bright ending and aromatics that just won't quit. Long Shadows Poet's Leap Dry Riesling from Columbia Valley is also impressive, as is Charles Smith Wines Kung Fu Girl Riesling, especially fermented and made to pair with Asian foods. Exceptional and fun. Not to leave out Oregon, Brooks Ara Riesling from the Willamette Valley is incredibly delicious.

Sauvignon Blanc

Sauvignon Blanc is a wine with great fresh-fruit flavors, as well as a zippy acidity that is bone-dry. My first love was Cakebread Cellars Sauvignon Blanc North Coast. I always wanted red wine, but then someone brought over this wine. I was instantly taken with it. It is made from grapes grown in the Napa Valley and the North Coast. It includes 5 percent Sémillon and 1 percent Sauvignon Musqué, and is made in stainless steel (97 percent), concrete eggs (2 percent), and older oak (1 percent). Most of it is aged in neutral oak barrels for five months. The result is an incredibly complex wine with immense flavor and wonderful layers.

My second favorite was introduced to me by wine writer Elizabeth Smith, from St. Clair Brown Winery & Brewery in Napa, the funkiest and perhaps best urban winery I have ever visited. Run by winemaker/brewmaster Elaine St. Clair and president Laina Brown, this boutique winery shines like crazy. Their Sauvignon Blanc is floral, aromatic, and thirst quenching.

In Oregon, there are three from the Willamette Valley that I love: J. Christopher Sauvignon Blanc, Andrew Rich Vintner Sauvignon Blanc Croft Vineyard, and King Estate Sauvignon Blanc. Plus there are River's Edge Sauvignon Blanc Vintage Farm Vineyard from Elkton and Patricia Green Cellars Estate Vineyard Sauvignon Blanc Ribbon Ridge AVA. From neighboring Washington, there's Watchful Maker Sauvignon Blanc and Jaine Evergreen Vineyard Sauvignon Blanc.

On the East Coast, on Long Island, Macari Vineyards' Sauvignon Blanc, without question, towers over the landscape. Both their Katherine's Field and Lifeforce (made in cement eggs) are stellar, with fruit that lasts and lasts and a complexity that constantly brings new flavors to the fore. Paumanok Sauvignon Blanc and Bedell Sauvignon Blanc are both eye-opening. McCall Sauvignon Blanc Cuvée Nicola is always a winner. All are located on the North Fork.

From New Jersey, William Heritage Sauvignon Blanc is super impressive, with big flavor and a lovely, bright finish. Saltwater Farm Vineyard Sauvignon Blanc from Stonington, Connecticut, is a stunner. Pennsylvania produces the very good Penns Woods Sauvignon Blanc. In Maryland, Boordy Vineyards Sauvignon Blanc Dry Bench Reserve is wonderful, as is the Sauvignon Blanc from Big Cork Vineyards. Pippin Hill Farm & Vineyards Sauvignon Blanc from the Monticello region of Virginia is impressive, as is Stinson Vineyards Sauvignon Blanc from the Blue Ridge Mountains, fermented in concrete and stainless steel. From Michigan, there are the outstanding Black Star Farms Arcturos Sauvignon Blanc and quaffable Modales Hollywood Vineyard Sauvignon Blanc Lake Michigan Shore. Messina Hof Sauvignon Blanc, grown at an elevation of 3,700 feet in the Texas High Plains, is very tasty.

Chardonnay

Chardonnay grows well almost across the country. The best producers come from California, though I also love what's being produced in New York and Virginia. Canada also offers some lovely Chardonnays.

The first Chardonnays that opened my eyes, from Kistler Vineyards and Pahlmeyer, were shared with me by friend and employer Buz Teacher. Kistler Vineyards Cuvée Cathleen Vineyard and Kistler Vineyards McCrea Vineyard Sonoma Mountain both have great minerality, huge mouthfeel, and lovely acidity. Pahlmeyer Chardonnay Napa Valley is almost the opposite—massively rich, opulent, and complex, with dried apricots, dried pineapple, and hints of lemon zest, caramel, and vanilla, and notes of brioche and shortbread, it is a supersized Chardonnay. But these are unicorn Chardonnays. Another big favorite, and much more accessible, is Grgich Hills Estate Chardonnay Napa Valley. A classic from the region.

Also from California are Flowers Sonoma Coast Chardonnay, MacRostie Chardonnay Sonoma Coast, Talbott Kali Hart Chardonnay from Carmel-by-the-Sea, Walter Hansel Family Vineyards Russian River Valley Chardonnay, Ramey Chardonnay Russian River Valley, and Schermeister Laura's Chardonnay Antica Vineyard Atlas Peak Napa Valley. Also, I absolutely love Fort Ross Mother of Pearl Chardonnay Fort Ross Vineyard. Fess Parker Ashley's Chardonnay Sta. Rita Hills is another one of my cellar favorites.

From Oregon I love Domaine Drouhin Arthur Chardonnay Dundee Hills, Stoller Family Estate Reserve Chardonnay, Irvine & Roberts Vineyards Estate Chardonnay Rogue Valley, and Durant Vineyards Lark Chardonnay. From Washington State, look for VanArnam Vineyards Chardonnay Yakima Valley, DAMA Wines Chardonnay from Walla Walla, and Reininger Reserve Chardonnay Stillwater Creek Vineyard Columbia Valley.

Some of my favorite Chardonnays come from New York: Wölffer Estate Perle Chardonnay, Lenz Old Vines Chardonnay, Paumanok Minimalist Chardonnay, and Channing Daughters Scuttlehole Chardonnay from Long Island. From the Finger Lakes I like Fox Run Vineyards Reserve Chardonnay Kaiser Vineyard, Trestle Thirty One Chardonnay, Lamoreaux Landing Reserve Chardonnay, and Osmote Seneca Lake Chardonnay.

Other East Coast notables include Unionville Vineyards Pheasant Hill Chardonnay from New Jersey, Boordy Vineyards Chardonnay Dry Bench Reserve from Maryland, and Penns Woods Chardonnay Reserve from Pennsylvania. Among Virginia offerings, I highly recommend Chatham Vineyards on Church Creek Chardonnay Steel from the Eastern Shore, Jefferson Vineyards Chardonnay, Barboursville Vineyards Chardonnay Reserve, and King Family Vineyards Chardonnay, both their Small Batch Stainless Steel and the barrel fermented.

Bachelder offers some of my favorite Chardonnays from Canada, with their "Les Villages" Niagara-on-the-Lake and "Les Villages" Bench and Niagara Escarpment Chardonnays, which are both exquisite. Another stellar choice is Flat Rock Cellars Chardonnay Twenty Mile Bench, a blend of tank- and barrel-fermented wines aged on the lees. It's flinty and zippy in the best possible ways. Tawse Quarry Road Chardonnay is another favorite. From the Okanagan Valley there are Quails' Gate Chardonnay Rosemary's Block, Meyer Family Vineyards Chardonnay McLean Creek Road Vineyard, and Cave Spring Chardonnay.

SECONDARY WHITES

Pinot Grigio

Pinot Grigio is among the best-selling whites in the United States, when you include the Italian bottlings. But few people realize how many Pinot Grigios are being made in North America these days. Part of it is confusion about Pinot Grigio and its French namesake, Pinot Gris. In Europe, Pinot Grigio is picked early, while the acidity is still quite high, and processed into a refreshing light wine. Sometimes flavor is sacrificed for acidity, but this does not mean the wines aren't wonderful. Pinot Gris, mainly grown in the Alsace region of France, tends to be left on the vines until much later in the season. There, they produce medium-bodied and even some full-bodied versions of this wine. While the Italian wines seem to focus on citrus and honeydew melon, the French wines tend to show more stone fruit and are more floral on the nose.

In North America, there seem to be no rules when it comes to this wine. Many of the larger manufacturers follow the Italian line, making lighter, more citrus-focused wines. And it seems there are more stylistic choices being made available by medium-sized and small artisanal wineries offering a vast array of finishes.

Pinot Blanc is a cousin of Pinot Grigio/Pinot Gris. All three are derived from Pinot Noir, where they get part of their name. Pinot Blanc tends to be finished in the same fashion as these other two—either in a lighter, zippier style or in a bigger-bodied way with more aromatics and fruit. Pinot Blanc has historically been grown in the Champagne and Burgundy regions of France.

On the East Coast, the North Fork produces several good versions, from Channing Daughters Pinot Grigio to Lenz Pinot Gris. In North Stonington, Connecticut, is Jonathan Edwards Estate Pinot Gris. There are several good Pinot Grigios from New Jersey: Hawk Haven Signature Series Dry Pinot Grigio Cape May, Auburn Road Pinot Grigio, and William Heritage Pinot Gris, the last two from the Outer Coastal Plain. Boordy Vineyards Pinot Grigio from Maryland is quite tasty, as is Bordeleau Lot 7 Pinot Grigio from Maryland's Eastern Shore. Barboursville Vineyards Virginia Pinot Grigio is as Italian as they come, not a surprise, since they are owned by the Italian wine giant Zonin.

Fenn Valley Vineyards makes a quaffable Pinot Grigio out of Michigan, as does Chateau Grand Traverse. Also recommended are the offerings from Ohio's Grand River Cellars and Texas's Llano Estacado Winery and Messina Hof Winery.

Oregon has become one of the premiere producers of Pinot Gris in the United States. There's Foris Pinot Gris Rogue Valley, but many of my favorites come from the Willamette Valley: Chehalem Pinot Gris, Cardwell Hill Cellars Estate Bottled Pinot Gris, Ponzi Vineyards Old Vine Pinot Gris, Archery Summit Vireton Pinot Gris, Evesham Wood Le Puits Sec Pinot Gris Eola—Amity Hills, The Eyrie Vineyards Estate Pinot Gris

Dundee Hills, Brooks Winery Estate Pinot Gris Eola–Amity Hills, and Sokol Blosser Winery Estate Pinot Gris Willamette Valley, among many others. You cannot go wrong with a Willamette Pinot Gris.

In California, there's J Vineyards Pinot Gris, Hess Persson Estates Select California Pinot Gris, Etude Pinot Gris Carneros, Robert Sinskey Vineyards Pinot Gris Los Carneros, Lichen Estate Pinot Gris Anderson Valley, and Jolie-Laide Pinot Gris California from Sonoma.

And don't forget Canada, with wines like Quails' Gate Three Wolves Pinot Gris, Sage Hills Winery & Organic Vineyards Pinot Gris, and Maverick Estate Winery Pinot Gris, all from Okanagan Valley, as well as Prince Edward Island's Norman Hardie County Pinot Gris.

Gewürztraminer

Gewürztraminer is one of my favorite white wines. It is super aromatic—a great wine by itself, as well as a terrific blender. A few drops of this wine in another wine immediately lifts the bouquet. The nose is packed with apricot, tangerine, pineapple, and lychee, as well as some honeysuckle and other floral notes. No matter how dry a Gewürztraminer is, it always has a note of sweetness. The best dry Gewürztraminers end with a hint of grapefruit and a long-lasting flavor of fruit and mouthwatering acidity.

There are many more Gewürztraminers available now than ever before, and the list seems to be growing. There are some really smashing offerings from the East Coast. Jonathan Edwards Gewürztraminer from North Stonington, Connecticut, comes to mind. In New York's Finger Lakes, try the Gewürztraminers from Dr. Konstantin Frank Winery, Standing Stone Vineyards, Ravines Wine Cellars, Lakewood Vineyards,

Keuka Spring Vineyards, Anthony Road Wine Company, and Sheldrake Point Winery, among others.

From California, try Gundlach Bundschu Dry Gewürztraminer, Union Sacré Wines Gewürztraminer Los Ositos Vineyard Arroyo Seco (an extended skin contact white wine), and Husch Anderson Valley Dry Gewürztraminer.

In Oregon, you can find Foris Dry Gewürztraminer Rogue Valley, Maloof Gewürztraminer Oak Ridge Vineyard, Ovum Keeper of the Flame Gewürztraminer Gerber Vineyard, Nehalem Bay Gewürztraminer, and Fossil & Fawn Gewürztraminer. In Washington State, I like Chateau Ste. Michelle Gewürztraminer and B. Lovely Gewürztraminer.

Canada also has a lot to offer, such as Jackson-Triggs Grand Reserve Gewürztraminer, Château des Charmes Gewürztraminer, and Reif Estate Winery Gewürztraminer. In the Bench region, you'll see plenty of lovely Riesling/Gewürztraminer blends.

Viognier

Originally made popular in the Rhône Valley in France, Viognier is another aromatic white that seems to have made great strides in the last ten to fifteen years in this country. Unlike Gewürztraminer, which tends to be a lighter white, Viognier can be made into whites as full-bodied as Chardonnay. It has an immensely perfumy nose, with floral notes, tropical fruits, and big fruit on the palate. It has established quite a foothold in California, Virginia, and Oregon. The grape is also grown to a lesser extent in Georgia, North Carolina, Texas, Washington, Michigan, Idaho, Colorado, New Mexico, Pennsylvania, Maryland, New Jersey, Missouri, and Arizona.

The Viognier I first fell in love with was from Jefferson Vineyards in the Monticello region of Virginia. I tried it on my first trip through the state, in a good glass, and the nose exploded. I was instantly captivated. The aromas are overwhelming, so filled with flowers and fruit that it can put some folks off. Not me! Other favorite Virginia vineyards for Viognier include Linden Vineyards, DuCard Vineyards, Barboursville Vineyards, Michael Shaps Wineworks, and Iron Will Winery. In New York State, there's Palmer Vineyards and Bedell Cellars, both of which offer excellent Viogniers. From Maryland, try Boordy Vineyards Landmark Dry Bench Reserve Viognier and Black Ankle Vineyards Viognier.

In New Jersey, Hawk Haven Vineyard Viognier and William Heritage Viognier are both very good. Penns Woods Viognier Reserve from Pennsylvania and St. Julian Winery's Braganini Reserve Viognier Lake Michigan Shore are lovely. From Texas, Becker Vineyards, Pedernales Cellars, McPherson Cellars, and Bent Oak Winery all get high marks for their Viogniers. La Chiripada Winery Artist Series 1 Viognier from New Mexico is elegant. Owner Larry Oddo at The Winery at Holy Cross Abbey makes a surprisingly good wine in Colorado.

One of my favorite California versions is Schermeister Viognier Salomon Vineyard Sonoma Valley, which I tasted at the winery. Stored in newish and older oak, this wine has big notes of guava and honeysuckle, and the fruit just lasts and lasts on the palate. I also like Jaffurs Viognier Bien Nacido Vineyard from the Santa Maria Valley. Fess Parker Rodney's Vineyard Viognier Santa Barbara County and Ampelos Viognier "Phi" Santa Barbara County are also memorable. Noteworthy offerings from Napa Valley include Stag's Leap Viognier, Freemark Abbey Viognier Napa Valley, and Darioush Signature Viognier.

Mark Ryan Winery Viognier from Washington State's Columbia Valley and K Vintners Viognier Art Den Hoed Vineyard Yakima Valley are both tasty. RoxyAnn Winery from Oregon makes a very drinkable Viognier.

I also like Penner-Ash Viognier, Cristom Viognier Louise Vineyard, King Estate Quail Run Vineyards Viognier, Kriselle Cellars Viognier, and Cowhorn Reserve Applegate Valley Viognier.

PRIMARY REDS

Pinot Noir

I did not have a big "aha!" moment with Pinot Noir. In my youth I was a fan of Cabernet Sauvignon and Zinfandel. I wanted Amarone and anything that was big and dark and tannic. But as I went along, I experienced Pinot Noir in a different kind of way.

I remember my first bottle of Kistler Vineyards Sonoma Coast Pinot Noir back in the late 1990s. Kistler is a Chardonnay house that makes a small amount of Pinot Noir. The vineyard sits on a ridge with the Sonoma Coast on one side, the Russian River Valley on the other. The wine is super concentrated, dark, and powerful, with immense fruit and a terrific nose. Dark red fruit and blueberry come through. It's made in open-top containers and aged for fourteen or so months before bottling. It's an absolutely wonderful wine.

Later in my career, I went to a Burgundy tasting and was shocked at the difference between these Pinot Noirs and their California brethren. They were so much lighter in color, more delicate in flavor.

Then I had Pinot Noir from the Niagara Bench, the first from Lailey Winery in Niagara-on-the-Lake, Ontario. This was another eye-opener. The wine was damn near a rosé, but I was taken with it. Not much later, I visited Tawse Winery and tried all three of their Pinot Noirs—Quarry Road, Vinemont Ridge, and Growers Blend. All were exceptional and more toward the Burgundy style.

Then came the coup de grâce that made Pinot Noir my favorite red wine. Over a three-year period, I visited and tasted the wines from many of the best Pinot Noir producers in the Santa Barbara, Santa Ynez, and Santa Rita Mountains, as well as the surrounding regions—Sea Smoke, Babcock, Brewer-Clifton, Jaffurs and I fell head over heels in love with the grape.

Later on, as winemakers, we got our first score of 90 points or better for our Hudson-Chatham Columbia County Pinot Noir, with grapes grown on the banks of the Hudson River. Like Kistler, we fermented open top, punching down twice a day, and aged the wine for sixteen months in neutral oak before bottling.

Bringing a successful Pinot Noir to harvest is among the biggest reliefs in winemaking. Cabernet Sauvignon and Merlot are tough as nails—they can withstand a lot. But not Pinot Noir—it is the heartbreak grape if you are a farmer. Thin-skinned, it is prone to disease and insect bites. It is the canary in the coal mine of grapes. In a vineyard, Pinot Noir will be the first of the grapes to attract whatever disease or insect or bird is coming down the line. In the East, the saying is, if you can grow peaches, you can grow Pinot Noir. But it's never that easy.

But, of course, I had fallen in love with Burgundy and Rhône-styled wines. We bought local Pinot Noir grapes and grew Baco Noir, Chelois, and Burden, all grapes whose wines are meant to emulate Pinot Noir (by and large). A fellow winemaker once attempted to criticize my Baco Noir by saying it tasted nothing like Baco Noir but was a very good Pinot Noir. I accepted that as a compliment. That wine became the first red hybrid wine ever to get a score of 90 points or better from any major wine publication. Ours happened to be from *Wine Enthusiast*.

In North America, my favorite growing regions for Pinot Noir are Santa Barbara, Oregon, Niagara-on-the-Bench, and New York State, though

I do love some offerings from Napa, Sonoma, and elsewhere. I like cool-climate Pinot Noirs. Hot-climate Pinot Noirs tend to taste out of balance to me.

I like the classic features of Pinot Noir—bright cherry and blueberry and a perfume of violets. These wines go great with salmon, tuna, and shark steaks, as well as roast chicken, pork, cheese, and other dishes. As I have gotten older, I tend to choose a Pinot Noir over all other reds.

My very favorite region for Pinot Noir is the area comprising Santa Barbara, Santa Maria Valley, Santa Rita Hills, and Santa Ynez Valley, and my very favorite wine is Sanford Pinot Noir from Sanford & Benedict Vineyard Sta. Rita Hills. Richard Sanford and Michael Benedict were partners from 1970 to 1980, then Sanford went off and founded Sanford Vineyards in 1980. A Vietnam War veteran, he was the first to plant Pinot Noir in the region. People thought him mad. Turned out he was as right as rain.

I love Sea Smoke Southing, Babcock Winery's Ghost Pinot Noir, Foley Sta. Rita Hills Rancho Santa Rosa Pinot Noir, Dierberg Pinot Noir Drum Canyon Vineyard, Fiddlehead Cellars Oregon Pinot Noir Oldsville Reserve and their Seven Twenty Eight Pinot Noir Fiddlestix Vineyard Sta. Rita Hills, Flying Goat Cellars Sta. Rita Hills Rio Vista Vineyard (and all their other Pinots), Zotovich Vineyards Estate Grown Pinot Noir, Brewer-Clifton Sta. Rita Hills Machado Pinot Noir, and Foxen Winery Julia's Vineyard Pinot Noir, among many others.

Elsewhere in California, there's Kistler Sonoma Coast, Schermeister's Pinot Noirs from the Sonoma Coast and Russian River Valley, Fort Ross

FRV Pinot Noir, and Williams Selyem Pinot Noir Sonoma Coast. These wines are in a whole other class—big and dark and impressive. Also look for J. Rochioli Pinot Noir, Aston Estate Pinot Noir, Paul Hobbs Pinot Noir Goldrock Estate Sonoma Coast, and Belle Glos Pinot Noir Clark & Telephone.

Oregon is my second-favorite producer. I love Durant Vineyards Madrone Pinot Noir and their La Casita Vineyard Pinot Noir, Sokol Blosser Big Tree Block Estate and their Orchard Block Estate Pinot Noirs, Stoller Winemaker's Series Whole Cluster Pinot Noir and their Dundee Hills Pinot Noir, Brooks Old Vine Pommard Pinot Noir and their Cahiers Pinot Noir, Irvine & Roberts Vineyards Estate Pinot Noir and their Convergence Pinot Noir and 777 Block Pinot Noir, RoxyAnn Winery Pinot Noir, Argyle Nuthouse Pinot Noir and many of their other bottlings, Domaine Drouhin (an extension of the exceptional Burgundy house) Pinot Noir Dundee Hills and their Laurène and Edition Limitée, Erath Fairsing Vineyard and their Willakia Vineyard Pinot Noirs, Ken Wright Cellars Pinot Noir, and many, many more.

In New York's Finger Lakes region, there are Heart & Hands Wine Company Mo Chuisle Estate Reserve Pinot Noir and their Charlie's Vineyard Reserve Estate Vineyard Pinot Noir, Dr. Konstantin Frank Old Vines Pinot Noir, Ravines Argetsinger Vineyard Pinot Noir, Nathan K. Pinot Noir, Lamoreaux Landing Pinot Noir, Heron Hill IV Pinot Noir, Fox Run Vineyards Pinot Noir, Red Tail Ridge Pinot Noir, Rooster Hill Estate Reserve Pinot Noir, Forge Cellars Pinot Noir Classique, and so many others.

On Long Island, look for McCall Reserve Pinot Noir and their Hillside Corchaug Estate Pinot Noir, Macari Pinot Noir, Lenz Pinot Noir, and Shared Table Farm Reserve Pinot Noir. In the Hudson Valley, Tousey Winery, Nostrano Vineyards, and Millbrook Vineyards & Winery all have notable offerings. On the Niagara Escarpment, I like Arrowhead Spring Reserve Pinot Noir.

From Ontario, I love Bachelder "Les Villages" Pinot Noir Niagara-on-the-Lake and their "Les Villages" Bench Pinot Noir Niagara Escarpment, as well as all the iterations of Pinot Noir at Tawse Winery. Lailey's Pinot Noir is light and delicate. Also wonderful are all the Pinot Noirs from Château des Charmes, including Cuvée Michèle Estate Grown, "Old Vines" Pinot Noir, and Paul Bosc Estate. Others to search out include Flat Rock Cellars Pinot Noir and their Gravity Pinot Noir, The Farm Wines Neudorf Vineyard Pinot Noir, and Southbrook Pinot Noir Laundry Vineyard Lincoln Lakeshore.

Other outliers that are worthy of note include the Pinot Noirs of Ankida Ridge Vineyards and Narmada Winery, both of Virginia, M Cellars of Ohio (amazing), and Penns Woods Reserve Pinot Noir of Pennsylvania.

Merlot

Merlot is a maligned grape; hugely popular in the 1980s and 1990s, it suffered a loss in reputation in the 2000s. Albeit, much of its demise lies at the feet of the oft-quoted lines, "I don't care. I'm not drinking Merlot!" from the movie *Sideways*. That's unfortunate.

The truth is, Merlot's toughest challenge is that it is the middle child of the red grape spectrum. What were its positive attributes forty years ago (darker and meatier than Pinot, not as abrasive as Cabernet Sauvignon or Zinfandel) make it a mealy-mouthed grape in today's market. In the current zeitgeist, if Cabernet Sauvignon is the stellar athlete or movie star, and Pinot Noir is a great artist, then Merlot is an accountant. But it's much more than that.

I don't think too many people think of a Merlot "region," when pressed. Of course, the West Coast produces plenty of it, and New York's North Fork is another source.

In California, there's no question, Duckhorn Vineyards Napa Valley Merlot (and their Three Palms Vineyard, especially) has always been one of the standard-bearers of the grape's ability to produce a sexy, sumptuous wine. Pahlmeyer Merlot is an absolute eye-opener. Cakebread Cellars Merlot Napa Valley is also special. Chappellet Napa Valley Merlot, Ehlers Estate Merlot, La Jota Vineyard Co., Howell Mountain Vineyards, Ridge Estate Merlot Santa Cruz Mountains, Ancient Peaks Paso Robles Merlot, Trefethen Oak Knoll District Merlot, Grgich Hills Estate Napa Valley Merlot Estate Grown, Austin Hope Merlot Paso Robles, and Freemark Abbey Merlot Napa Valley are Merlots that I enjoy immensely.

L'Ecole No. 41 Merlot Columbia Valley (and their Estate Ferguson & Seven Hills Vineyards Merlot) in Washington State is one of the great American Merlots. Chateau Ste. Michelle Canoe Ridge Estate Merlot is a special wine, as well as several of their other Merlot offerings. Two Mountain Copeland Vineyard Merlot, Cultura Merlot, Leonetti Cellar Merlot, Columbia Crest Reserve Shaw Red Mountain Merlot, Long Shadows Pedestal Merlot, and Barnard Griffin Merlot are all excellent wines.

In New York, Long Island offers a number of great Merlots. One of my absolute favorites is from Lenz, a classic French-styled Merlot, elegant, layered, and complex. Bedell Merlot is also a great choice. I like Christian's Cuvée Merlot and The Grapes of Roth Merlot from Wölffer Estate on the South Fork. Paumanok Merlot, Pellegrini Vineyards Merlot, and Macari Merlot Reserve are other Long Island favorites.

Cabernet Sauvignon

For more than half a century in America, Cabernet Sauvignon has been the lightning rod of wines. The victory of Warren Winiarski's Stag's Leap Winery Cabernet Sauvignon in the "Judgment of Paris" served as its coming-out party. Its triumph was the result of over a decade's hard work by winemakers like California wine evangelist Robert Mondavi.

But Cabernet Sauvignon's zeitgeist also proved to be its downfall. In the late 1990s and early 2000s, many in the industry changed their wine-making techniques in order to curry favor with *Wine Advocate* writer/editor/publisher Robert Parker. Parker favored big, dark, concentrated Cabs with high alcohol, which required cold soaks and massive manip-ulation. Those slow to budge, or unwilling to, were punished by being ignored. Corporate suits demanded that wine profiles change to meet Parker's unspoken but quite obvious standards.

When the first few wines of this type came out, they were indeed revo-lutionary and different, and produced in small runs. But like the NFL, the wine industry is a copycat league. And so hundreds of California wineries were soon aping the style, seeking to achieve high scores from Parker. In the process, winemaking of finesse and elegance gave way to what would ultimately be termed "big-dick bottles."

The 1990s and 2000s saw heavy bottles full of 15 and 16 percent al-cohol wines, compared to the 12 to 13.5 percent alcohol wines of Bor-deaux and elsewhere. The most famous incident during this period was when Tim Mondavi was relieved of winemaking responsibilities in his family's namesake company because he would not make the powerful wines that Parker (and now other magazines) required. Suits needed reviews to get wholesalers and stores to buy the wines. But even as the wine media's scores began declining in influence (because a whole new generation of wine drinkers was losing interest in them), there were whole lines of wines being made specifically for investment bankers and tech executives to buy and brag about.

Where was I in all this? Guilty as charged. I was taken by the new big wines, but I also knew they were a novelty run amok. In the beginning I couldn't get enough of them. But then I realized, with their 15 percent alcohol, they were tough to swallow. Soon I was reaching for slightly lighter wines, leaving a lot of the Cabernet Sauvignons to collect dust in the cellar. I still love a good glass of Cabernet Sauvignon, but it is the sledgehammer of the wine world, with big, dark fruits, tannins, complexity. I don't eat steak every day and I don't drink Cabernet Sauvignon every day.

If you don't like oak, Cabernet Sauvignon is not for you. With its big, bold flavors, Cabernet Sauvignon needs time to round down and find its place. A Cab remarkably transforms after twelve to sixteen months in French oak.

With their robust profile, many Cabernet Sauvignons are perfect for any kind of roast beast, as well as big, powerful dishes like penne arrabbiata. Its fruit, acids, and tannins cut through the most flavorful foods. That's why rich Italian cheeses and charcuterie pair so beautifully with it.

Cabernet Sauvignon is the most popularly planted vine in the world. California is a great place to grow it because of the long growing season, with more days of sunshine, which produce more mature berries by the time of harvest. If Cabernet Sauvignon is picked before it is fully ripe, the resulting varietal wine screams of green bell pepper.

When you drink this wine, you're hanging out with the big boys. The better wines cost more. In the recommendations that follow, I've included some midpriced bottles, but Cabernet Sauvignon is almost always the highest-priced wine in a winery's portfolio.

The first big Cabernet Sauvignon I remember drinking that still holds up for me is Cakebread Cellars Cabernet Sauvignon Napa Valley. I also like their Suscol Springs and Vine Hill Ranch bottlings but the classic Cakebread is still my favorite. The wine is 90 percent or more Cabernet Sauvignon, with small dollops of Merlot, Petit Verdot, and Malbec in descending order, percentagewise. The grapes are cold soaked before pressing, "which softens the grape skins and further helps extract color and tannin," says the winemaker's notes. The wine is usually aged seventeen to eighteen months in new French oak and neutral oak after fermentation is complete.

Stag's Leap Artemis Napa Valley was my next eye-opening experience. Like the Cakebread, Artemis offers notes of mocha and dark red fruit. Blackberry, dark cherry, and dark raspberry with a hint of cassis and dark chocolate notes make it a wonderful wine.

Another big favorite is Beaulieu Vineyard Georges de Latour Private Reserve Cabernet Sauvignon, which was among the first important modern Cabernet Sauvignons, created by the great André Tchelistcheff in 1936. He was the first winemaker in Napa Valley to approach wine scientifically. He was easily the most influential winemaker in America post-Prohibition and brought California wine into the modern age. The tree of winemakers whom he taught is exhausting to trace. Not only is the wine fantastic—deep, rich, and layered—but every time I drink Georges de Latour, it feels like drinking history. That he and Dr. Konstantin Frank of the Finger Lakes (who brought vinifera to the East Coast) were such good friends (both Russian émigrés) is yet another perk of wine history. Georges de Latour was the man who founded Beaulieu Vineyard back in the early 1900s. Trevor Durling, only the fifth winemaker in the company's 119-year history (he's been there more than a decade himself), coal soaks for seven to ten days. The wines are put into special tanks that have their own centrifugal pump to ferment on the skins. These automated tanks ensure that the cap keeps moving, constantly being broken up without overextraction.

I also like Charles Krug Cabernet Sauvignon. Krug is the oldest continually operating winery in Napa Valley, founded in 1882. Krug's wine is mainly made from grapes harvested from their five family estates in Yountville (they also have an exceptional Family Reserve Howell Mountain bottling). I love the fruit in this wine, with lots of bright cherry and hints of strawberry and fresh raspberry, as well as lovely mocha and dark chocolate notes.

Other favorites include Madrigal Family Cabernet Sauvignon Napa Valley, Ehlers Estate Cabernet Sauvignon Napa Valley, Chappellet Signature Cabernet Sauvignon, Pahlmeyer Proprietary Red (88 percent Cabernet Sauvignon, 11 percent Merlot, and 1 percent Cabernet Franc), Chateau Montelena Cabernet Sauvignon Napa Valley, Austin Hope Paso Robles Cabernet Sauvignon, Mount Veeder Winery Cabernet Sauvignon Napa Valley, Spring Mountain Vineyard Cabernet Sauvignon, and Daou Reserve Cabernet Sauvignon Paso Robles (they have numerous releases, all of which are very good, but this is their affordably priced version).

Washington State also produces wonderful Cabernet Sauvignons. Certainly, my favorite is L'Ecole No. 41 Cabernet Sauvignon Columbia Valley. Chateau Ste. Michelle Cabernet Sauvignon is a best buy (hands down). They have numerous bottlings. Their Red Mountain Cabernet Sauvignon is something special. Long Shadows Feather Cabernet Sauvignon, Hedges Family Estate Red Mountain Cabernet Sauvignon, Kiona Estate Bottled Red Mountain Cabernet Sauvignon (Kiona has the second-oldest vines in the state), and Bledsoe Family Winery Cabernet Sauvignon Walla Walla Valley and their higher-end Doubleback Cabernet Sauvignon are all worth seeking out.

From Texas, there are a few Cabernet Sauvignons of note, including Messina Hof Paulo Cabernet Sauvignon, Becker Vineyards Iconoclast, and Ron Yates Cabernet Sauvignon Friesen Vineyards. Also try New York

State's Lenz Old Vines Cabernet Sauvignon and Paumanok Limited Edition Cabernet Sauvignon Tuthills Lane Vineyard.

SECONDARY REDS

Cabernet Franc

This grape has come on strong in the last twenty years in the United States. There are good Cabernet Francs being produced in many regions, from Massachusetts down to the Carolinas, west to Ohio and Michigan, and up and down the West Coast. It is without question the hot new red. It's hardier, with a better chance of ripening than Cabernet Sauvignon.

There are winemakers attempting to create Bordeaux-like wines from Cabernet Franc. Some are very good; however, like other grapes, you can push Cabernet Franc only so far. In warm regions with lots of sunny days, if done well, Cabernet Franc can approach such heights (with small additions of Petit Verdot, Malbec, and Cabernet Sauvignon). These wines can exhibit notes of bright and dark cherry, raspberry, and plum.

In New England and down through New Jersey, there are a number of wineries making more Loire-ish Cabernet Francs, lighter in style (like a Pinot Noir or Syrah), not aged in oak, that give off fresher fruit and are easier to drink. The notes on these wines include bright cherry, even hints of strawberry and red cassis.

As a winemaker, I saw too many East Coast and Midwest wineries trying to turn Cabernet Franc into Cabernet Sauvignon. It does not work. You can make an elegant dark wine out of it if you have the right weather. No problem. But, as a winemaker on the East Coast, I tried not to over-extract the wine, with the goal being a lighter-styled stainless steel and/or neutral oak version that was heavier than Pinot Noir but not as big as Cabernet Sauvignon. I loved making this wine.

There are a number of excellent wines in both camps. However, no one place highlights both approaches better than Macari Vineyards on the North Shore of Long Island. Their Cabernet Franc Lifeforce is aged in concrete eggs; it never touches wood. Lean and streamlined, this fresh, delicious Cab Franc is bright with ripe cherry and hints of red raspberries. The winery also offers a bigger, more complex Reserve, which rests in oak, with ripe dark cherry, dark raspberry, and lovely tannins. A beautiful, complex red with a lot going on. It's the only winery where I have seen both styles living side by side.

If I were to pick one bottle as the best example of the bigger, more full-bodied style, it would be Ehlers Estate Cabernet Franc. The historic winery was founded in 1886 but was left moribund after Prohibition, until it was rechristened Ehlers Estate around the turn of the century. Their Cabernet Franc is a big bowl of cherries, strawberries, and blackberries, chewy and delicious, ruby colored, with bright highlights. It is jammy, almost like a Malbec, a unique wine, the way only California can do it. The closest I have come to tasting a similar wine on the East Coast is Bedell Cabernet Franc from the North Fork. Slightly lighter, and aged in older neutral French oak, Bedell offers the same jammyness and structure. Two truly exceptional wines.

For California, I suggest Madrigal Family Winery Cabernet Franc, Charles Krug Cabernet Franc, Duckhorn Vineyards Cabernet Franc, Sequoia Grove Tonella Vineyard Cabernet Franc, Gundlach Bundschu Winery Cabernet Franc, Trefethen Family Vineyards Oak Knoll Vineyard Cabernet Franc, Austin Hope Cellar Select Cabernet Franc, Kenzo Estate Asuka Cabernet Franc, Alexander Valley Vineyards Estate Cabernet Franc, Jarvis Estate Cabernet Franc (Cave Fermented), Titus Napa Valley Cabernet Franc, Crocker & Starr St. Helena Cabernet Franc, and Jacob Franklin (Elyse) Cabernet Franc Napa Valley.

In Washington State, there are L'Ecole No. 41 Cabernet Franc Estate Ferguson & Seven Hills Vineyards Walla Walla Valley, DAMA Wines Cabernet Franc (with a few other very good bottlings), and Spring Valley Vineyard Katherine Corkum Cabernet Franc Walla Walla Valley. In Oregon, I like Leah Jørgensen Grand Reserve Cabernet Franc Applegate Valley.

Up and down the East Coast, Cabernet Franc has become the premiere red wine. From New England, there's Greenvale Cabernet Franc from Rhode Island, and two from Connecticut—Sharpe Hill Estate Cabernet Franc and Jonathan Edwards Estate Cabernet Franc. In New Jersey, I especially like Working Dog Winery Cabernet Franc Estate Bottled and Alba Vineyard Heritage Cabernet Franc. I very much enjoy Wölffer Estate Caya Cabernet Franc from Long Island, and in the Finger Lakes, the Shaw Vineyard Cabernet Franc Reserve. The Hudson Valley produces several very fine ones, including Robibero Estate Cabernet Franc, Quartz Rock Vineyard Cabernet Franc Estate Hudson River Region, and Benmarl Winery Cabernet Franc Estate. In Virginia, there are Veritas Cabernet Franc Monticello, Glen Manor Cabernet Franc, Jake Busching Cabernet Franc Barrel Aged, Fabbioli Cellars Cabernet Franc, and many others.

From Michigan, check out the Black Star Farms Arcturos Cabernet Franc, St. Julian Winery's Braganini Reserve Cabernet Franc Lake Michigan Shore, and Domaine Berrien Cellars Lake Michigan Shore Cab Franc.

The best versions of the lighter style include Fjord Vineyards Estate Cabernet Franc in the Hudson Valley, Hermann J. Wiemer Vineyard Cabernet Franc, Forge Cellars Willow Seneca Lake Cabernet Franc, Billsboro

Cabernet Franc from the Finger Lakes, and Unionville Vineyards Silver Lining Cabernet Franc from New Jersey.

Canadian versions include such Ontario offerings as Tawse Grower's Blend Cabernet Franc, Southbrook Triomphe Cabernet Franc, Stratus Cabernet Franc Niagara-on-the-Lake, Two Sisters Niagara River, and Konzelmann Estate Winery Family Reserve Cabernet Franc. From the Okanagan Valley, try the offerings from Poplar Grove Winery, Mission Hill Family Estate Winery, and Burrowing Owl Estate Winery.

Syrah

Syrah (also spelled Sirah) was popularly known to be a grape of great use in France in the Rhône Valley, where it is used in the Hermitage, Cornas, and Côtie-Rôtie in the northern regions, and Châteauneuf-du-Pape, Gigondas, and Côtes du Rhône in the southern regions. It is grown throughout Europe, as well as in Argentina, Chile, Uruguay, New Zealand, and South Africa. In Australia it is known as Shiraz. Syrah is among the top ten most planted wine grapes in the world.

In the United States, Syrah is grown in many regions, but most notably in California, Washington (near Walla Walla), Oregon, Ohio, and the mid-Atlantic states. Like many grapes, the varietal wines produced from Syrah can range from notes of dark cherry and blackberry, with hints of dark chocolate and black pepper, to lighter notes of blueberries, bright cherries, and plum, with hints of white pepper. I like both.

In what I consider the best Syrah region in the United States, Washington, I love Two Mountain Syrah, J Bell Cellars Red Mountain Syrah, VanArnam Vineyards Estate Reserve Syrah, Gård Syrah Grand Klasse Reserve, Reininger Helix Syrah Phinny Hill Vineyard, L'Ecole No. 41 Syrah Columbia Valley, and Long Shadows Vintners Collection Sequel Syrah Columbia Valley.

In Oregon, I really enjoy Abacela Syrah from the Umpqua Valley, Penner-Ash Syrah (sourced from southern and northern vineyards within in Oregon), Dobbes Family Estate Syrah Rogue Valley, and Brooks Terue Syrah Deux Vert Vineyard Willamette Valley.

In California, some of my favorites include Schermeister Scavenger Syrah Sonoma Valley and Ramey Rodgers Creek Vineyard Syrah Sonoma Coast, Peay Les Titans Estate Syrah Sonoma Coast, and Dehlinger Syrah Goldridge Vineyard Russian River Valley. Great examples from other regions in California include Doffo Winery Unfiltered Syrah and Chapin Private Reserve Syrah, both from Temecula, the Syrahs from Beckmen Vineyards in Los Olivos, Jaffurs Syrah Santa Barbara County, and Zotovich Estate Syrah Sta. Rita Hills.

In New York, there's Clovis Point Syrah, Bedell Syrah, and Lieb Cellars Syrah, all from Long Island, as well as Red Newt Glacier Ridge Vineyards Syrah and Billsboro Syrah from the Finger Lakes, and Arrowhead Spring Vineyards Syrah from the Niagara Escarpment. Some outliers include Black Ankle Vineyards Syrah and Catoctin Breeze Syrah from Maryland, as well as Hawk Haven Reserve Syrah and William Heritage Reserve Syrah from New Jersey. Carboy Winery and The Winery at Holy Cross Abbey offer excellent examples in Colorado, as do Llano Estacado Winery and Texas Legato Winery in Texas. There is also Blenheim Vineyards Syrah in Virginia and Domaine Berrien Cellars Syrah Lake Michigan Shore.

Zinfandel

Like many people, I got interested in Zinfandel in the late 1980s. Ravenswood, Rombauer, and Rosenblum were three of the big producers. I was a Ravenswood man. As senior editor Tim Fish in *Wine Spectator* says, "The value-priced Vintner's Blend Zinfandel provided the cash, and the single vineyard, old-vine Zins like Teldeschi, Old Hill and Dickerson provided the prestige."

And that's exactly the trajectory I followed. I started out with the Vintner's Blend, and then began buying the single vineyard Zins when I was making a little more money. I absolutely loved the Ravenswood Zins. The wines were super dark and rich, jam-packed with dark fruits like blackberry, dark raspberry, and cassis, with big tannins at the back. Perfect for rich, hard cheeses, spicy pasta dishes, or beef.

The biggest and best producer of Zinfandels is California. Some of my favorites include those from Turley Wine Cellars, Grgich Hills Estate, Madrigal Family Winery, and Martinelli, as well as Williams Selyem Russian River Valley Papera Vineyard Zinfandel, Bacigalupi Vineyards Zinfandel, Dry Creek Vineyard Old Vine Zinfandel, Ridge Pagani Ranch Zinfandel, Robert Biale Vineyards Black Chicken Zinfandel, Chateau Montelena Calistoga Zinfandel, Heitz Cellar Napa Valley Zinfandel, and Seghesio Family Vineyards Zinfandel Home Ranch Vineyard Alexander Valley. Matt Parish "The 24" Zinfandel Contra Costa County and their Louie's Block Old Vine Zinfandel are both excellent.

The Pines 1852 Old Vine Zinfandel Columbia Gorge and Sineann Old Vine Zinfandel Columbia Valley of Oregon are very good. Kuhlman Cellars Texas Zinfandel Escondido Valley is the best of its kind in Texas, as is Buckel Family Wine Zinfandel in Colorado.

TEN OBSCURE WHITE GRAPES TO TRY

Like many, I grew up on the classic whites—Chardonnay, Pinot Grigio, Sauvignon Blanc, etc. I cut my teeth on Blue Nun sweet Riesling. I was so proud the first year I brought a bottle of it to Thanksgiving. My Italian parents were horrified, but also amused. My next big find was DiGrazia Vineyards Autumn Spice, from Brookfield, Connecticut, a Vidal Blanc blend with pumpkin spice.

However, as I grew up, I looked for unique whites. In truth, it took time for me to come to Chardonnay, which most people do not realize is, in fact, the biggest of white wines. Like Cabernet Sauvignon, sometimes having Chardonnay with a dish is like carrying a sledgehammer when what you need is a tack hammer.

My first eye-opening experience with a unique white was discovering really terrific Vidal Blancs from Carolyn's Sakonnet Vineyard and Greenvale Vineyards in Rhode Island. The Greenvale was a stainless-steel version of the wine with tropical and lovely green apple notes. Bright and fresh. The Sakonnet Vidal Blanc was aged lightly in oak, giving more of a feel of a Fumé Blanc (which is a Sauvignon Blanc that usually has some light aging). It was green and bright, with notes of toast, vanilla, and fresh-cut ripe apple. I remember pouring it at one wine dinner after another, my guests shocked at the quality and impressive flavor of the wine. And to them, wine geeks all, an unheard-of grape.

Here are some of the lesser-known white grape wines you should try. They will increase your understanding of wine and how their flavors can impress.

Albariño

Whether you write it Albariño (Galician) or Alvarinho (Portuguese), the grape and the wine are associated with Galicia, in northwest Spain, though the grape is thought to have been brought there from the Rhine. Alba-Riño roughly translates as "white [wine] from the Rhine." Some experts believe it to be a Riesling, possibly from the Alsace region of France. Some scientists think it is more closely related genetically to the French grape Petit Manseng. Whatever its origins, Albariño is fast becoming one of the hottest alternative whites on the market.

My first experience with American-grown Albariño was with Old Westminster Winery in Maryland. A Maryland Albariño? Yep. The three principals of Old Westminster Winery are the Baker siblings, Drew, Lisa Hinton, and Ashli. In addition to managing their estate vines, they work closely with local winegrowers to source other grapes that reflect their region's unique geology and mesoclimate.

Old Westminster's Albariño is highly aromatic, somewhat akin to Viognier and Petit Manseng, both of which are popularly grown in Virginia, but the taste is much more akin to Riesling or Sauvignon Blanc. This light, brisk, almost clear wine has big whiffs of apricot, peach, and tropical fruit. Zippy and refreshing, it abounds with acidity. A wonderful food wine.

Another noteworthy maker is Abacela in the Umpqua Valley of southern Oregon, which produces an aromatic, fresh version of this wine. Other tasty Oregon versions of Albariño come from Tekstura Wine Co., Beacon Hill Winery & Vineyard, Analemma Wines, Ransom Wines, and Awen Winecraft.

Though Texas is mostly known for other white grapes, there are a number of very, very drinkable Albariños from there, including Pedernales Cellars Six Generations Albariño, McPherson Cellars, Wildseed Farms, English Newsom Cellars, and Ron Yates Wines, among others.

Fenestra Winery of Livermore Valley, in California, produces a terrific version. Greenvale Vineyards of Rhode Island makes an Albariño with a slight, slight hint of salinity (reflecting the winery's proximity to the Atlantic) that is bright and refreshing, with notes of lemon and lime. They offer it as a still wine and a sparkling Pét Nat.

Possibly one of my favorites is Matt Spaccarelli's and Casey Erdmann's Fjord Vineyards Albariño from the Hudson Valley, which is filled with fresh tropical fruit and Granny Smith green apple.

New Jersey produces several different versions, including Todd Wuerker's Hawk Haven Albariño (he has also done a Pét Nat version). Located near Cape May, it exhibits bright fruit and a hint of salinity. I also like Seferino Cotzojay's White Horse Winery Estate Albariño, which exudes big fruit and big flavors, possibly from its slightly extended extraction. Both are excellent. Long Island offers several, including those from Bedell Cellars, Palmer Vineyards, and Wölffer Estate Vineyard, all of which are exceptional. Like Hawk Haven, these island wineries have wonderful tropical fruit, fresh green apple, and a hint of salinity. The Finger Lakes offers the bright and refreshing Billsboro Albariño from the famed Sawmill Creek Vineyards.

Wineries like Blenheim Vineyards, Afton Mountain Vineyards, Chrysalis Vineyards, and Fifty-Third Winery and Vineyard in Virginia all offer stunning Albariños.

Chenin Blanc

Chenin Blanc is one of the most planted white varieties on the globe and is associated with some of the world's great wine regions, including the Loire Valley in France. Wine has been made from Chenin Blanc since the 1500s. In addition to France, it is planted in Spain, Australia, China, New Zealand, Canada, Argentina, South Africa, and the United States. However, while Chenin Blanc is a dominant grape around the world, it is less so in the United States. It's blended into a number of wines, but singular bottlings of fine wine are not as prevalent here as elsewhere. But that doesn't mean you shouldn't be drinking it.

One of my favorite versions comes from the Santa Barbara region in California. Foxen Vineyard & Winery, owned by Bill Wathen and Dick Doré, has been producing cool-climate wines since the mid-1980s. It's my favorite type of winery—small production, sustainably farmed, with a focus on the vineyards and an eye toward "minimalist" winemaking. Their Chenin Blanc has notes of ripe pear and fresh-cut apples, with hints of spice and a refreshing acidity on the end. The fruit lingers.

Other notable California offerings include Batik Chenin Blanc, Dry Creek Dry Chenin Blanc, Leo Steen Chenin Blanc Saini Farms Dry Creek Valley, Chalone Vineyard Estate Grown Chenin Blanc, and Pax Mahle Lyman Ranch Chenin Blanc Amador County, and two from Clarksburg, The Hobo Wine Company Folk Machine Chenin Blanc Merritt Island and Clarksburg Wine Company Chenin Blanc.

Chateau Ste. Michelle Limited Release Chenin Blanc from Washington State is another excellent example, as is L'Ecole No. 41 Yakima Valley Chenin Blanc Old Vines. Rhinory Chenin Blanc, McPherson Chenin Blanc Texas High Plains, Westcave Cellars Chenin Blanc, Lewis Wines Chenin Blanc Texas High Plains, and Pheasant Ridge Old Vine Chenin Blanc are very good offerings from Texas.

In the East, there are some impressive versions, including those from Kareem Massoud's outstanding Paumanok Vineyards on the North Fork on Long Island, William Heritage Winery in New Jersey, and Walsh Family Wine's Bethany Ridge Vineyard in Virginia.

Canada has some lovely examples as well: Reif Estate Winery Chenin Blanc and Big Head Chenin Blanc BA from Eastern Canada, and from the Okanagan Valley there are Inniskillin Discovery Series Chenin Blanc Okanagan Valley, Quails' Gate Chenin Blanc, and Okanagan Crush Pad Narrative Chenin Blanc. Try Road 13 Sparkling Chenin Blanc for a little something different.

Frontenac Gris

Frontenac Gris was released by the University of Minnesota in 2003. It is a cold-hardy grape, able to withstand brutal temperature drops in cold-climate regions and return with vigor the following season. According to the university, "The 'gris' in the name Frontenac gris is a nod to the gray color of the skin of these grapes. The pink-berried variant produces wine with a characteristic peach flavor." Frontenac Gris is usually produced in the stainless-steel style.

Petoskey Farms Estate Frontenac Gris Top of the Mitt is a wonderful light, aromatic wine with intense tropical notes and bright acidity. The Frontenac Gris from 7 Vines Vineyard of Minnesota has won many prestigious competitions and exhibits super-bright fruits, with lots of citrus and honey, and good acidity. Balanced Rock Winery is a solid Wisconsin producer. Coyote Moon Vineyards and Hudson-Chatham Winery both offer versions of this grape in New York State, as does Nimble Hill Winery & Brewery in Pennsylvania. Taylor Brooke Winery in Connecticut and Galena Cellars Vineyard & Winery in Illinois have lovely sparkling versions that are fun, easy drinking.

Grüner Veltliner

Grüner Veltliner is grown mostly in Austria, Hungary, Slovakia, and the Czech Republic, but in the last decade a number of regions in the United States and Canada have taken up the grape, including Pennsylvania, Massachusetts, Maryland, Oregon, Washington, California, and Michigan, as well as in the Okanagan Valley.

When I am with any of my wine writer friends, a surefire way to impress them is to pull out a bottle of Galen Glen Winery's Grüner Veltliner. Located in Andreas, Pennsylvania, Galen Glen produces some stellar wines, but none is more stunning or praiseworthy than their Grüner Veltliner. It is a big, perfumy citrus bomb with lime, lemon, and grapefruit. The grapefruit just explodes. Hints of nectarine. I also love the shock of white pepper at the end. Another very good version comes from Nimble Hill Winery, outside of Scranton.

New York State wineries producing super-drinkable Grüner Veltliner include One Woman Wines (North Fork), Heron Hill (Finger Lakes), Six Eighty Cellars (in a Pét Nat version), and Winery of Ellicottville. Maryland's Loew Vineyards and The Wine Collective (an urban winery in Baltimore) both offer excellent versions.

Westport Rivers Vineyard, located on the south coast of Massachusetts, not far from Buzzards Bay, offers a strikingly good Grüner, much bigger bodied than I have experienced with this grape, owing to slightly more grape skin contact than other whites. This is a robust white wine. I brought it to a fish dinner with shrimp in a creamy garlic sauce and grilled monkfish. It dazzled. Despite being pitted against more famous California names, it was the clear winner that night.

Michigan also produces some lovely Grüner Veltliners, including St. Julian Winery's dry Braganini Reserve Grüner Veltliner. It is light and bright with Granny Smith apple and Meyer lemon and terrific acidity. Other noteworthy offerings include Chateau Grand Traverse Grüner Veltliner, Shady Lane Cellars Grüner Veltliner Hennessy Vineyard Leelanau Peninsula, and Mari Vineyards Blackletter Grüner Veltliner Grishaw Vineyard Old Mission Peninsula.

Out West, the grape is now grown in Washington, Oregon, and California. Oregon has had some real successes, including Reustle Hefeabzug Estate Grüner Veltliner from the Umpqua Valley. Super minerality with hints of saline lurking behind big fruit. Ribbon Ridge Winery Ridgecrest Estate Grüner Veltliner, from the Willamette Valley, is aged for five months in a combination of concrete egg and neutral French oak. Fresh-cut peaches come straight out. Flâneur Wines Grüner Veltliner, from the Chehalem Mountains, exhibits fresh-cut young pears and lots of berries in the background. Chehalem Grüner Veltliner, from the Laurelwood District of the Willamette Valley, is a bright, zippy, mouth-grabbing wine, made fifty/fifty in neutral French and stainless steel.

Washington also offers excellent versions of the wine. Columbia Gorge has three exceptional Grüners: Savage Grace Underwood Mountain Vineyard Grüner Veltliner, Syncline Grüner Veltliner Bloxom Vineyard, and W.T. Vintners Underwood Mountain Vineyard Grüner Veltliner. Two other notables from Columbia Valley are Balboa Grüner Veltliner and Chateau Ste. Michelle Limited Release Grüner Veltliner.

California produces Luna Hart Grüner Veltliner, Summer Somewhere Kick On Ranch Vineyard Grüner Veltliner, and Lincourt Vineyards Grüner Veltliner from Sta. Rita Hills, all tasty choices.

La Crescent

La Crescent is another of the University of Minnesota's cold-climate grapes. Scientists James Luby and Peter Hemstad bred the vine, and the university was granted a US patent for it in 2004. The grapes were soon being shipped everywhere.

Vermont wine scribe and friend Todd Trzaskos and Montreal wine denizen Rémy Charest visited me at my home in the Hudson Valley and shared with me (and Hudson-Chatham winemaker J. Stephen Casscles) an exquisite bottle of Domaine La Garagista Vinu Jancu Vermont La Crescent. A massive treat! La Garagista owners Deirdre Heekin and Caleb Barber make this wine. "Vinu jancu" is the old Sicilian term for white wines made in the orange style, and this is an orange wine, made from Vermont-grown La Crescent, the grapes picked and sorted by hand, then pressed like red grapes and the wine aged on the skins. The resulting wine has a big mouthfeel. It is a chewy white filled with apricot, Seville oranges and orange blossoms, dried pineapple, and other tropical notes. It also has a great deal of acidity. The wine is perfectly balanced, immensely layered, and intricately flavored.

Another amazing La Crescent orange wine from Vermont is Shelburne Vineyard Iapetus Tectonic. Made by Joseph Ethan, this is a spectacular wine made through extended contact with the skins. With floral notes, the wine features flavors of a tart marmalade of apricot, tangerine, and orange, tinged with notes of honeydew melon.

In New York State, Gerry and Mary Barnhart's winery, Victory View, located north of Albany, produces stellar wines, including two La Crescents wines. Abigail is a semisweet classic wine with great balance and super acidity. Rae is an excellent orange wine, the wine and skins macerated for five days in stainless steel before pressing. Fossil Stone Vineyards La Crescent, also from the Upper Hudson Valley, is another exceptional version.

Bent Ladder's semisweet La Crescent hails from Doylestown, Ohio. Mousse Sparkling Wine Co. La Crescent from Minnesota has taken the local wine world by storm. The sweet notes are balanced by zippy acidity and great bubbles. But it was Sovereign Estate La Crescent that won the 2022 Minnesota Governor's Cup. Rustic Roots Winery's semisweet La Crescent from Scandia is an extremely popular wine, as is Grandview Valley Winery's La Crescent. Drumlin Ridge Winery La Crescent and 44's La Crescent are nice offerings from Wisconsin. The Carboy Winery at Mt. Garfield Estate Vineyard in Grand Valley, Colorado, also puts out a very impressive sparkling version.

Rkatsiteli

Rkatsiteli is an ancient vinifera grape that originated in the country of Georgia, and the name of the grape means "red stem." The grape has been dated back as far as 3000 BC. By the late 1970s, Rkatsiteli had become the main workhorse of the Soviet Union's wine industry. Today, the vine is planted in Russia, Armenia, Bulgaria, Moldova, Romania, North Macedonia, Azerbaijan, and Ukraine, as well as Australia and China. In the United States, New York's Finger Lakes region is the leader in production, but it can also be found in Massachusetts, New Jersey, Virginia, North Carolina, California, and Colorado. The resulting elegant wine makes for a floral nose, with great acidity and fruit, including apricot, pineapple, and honeydew, with spices like ginger and pepper.

The first Rkatsiteli I ever tasted was poured for me by Fred Frank of Dr. Konstantin Frank Winery on Keuka Lake in the Finger Lakes. Dr. Frank was the first to successfully grow vinifera wines on the East Coast. He is possibly one of the two or three most important people in the history of East Coast winemaking. Having come to the US from Russia in the 1950s, Dr. Frank was the first to plant Rkatsiteli in the Finger Lakes when he founded his winery in 1962. It is an elegant dry wine presenting a bouquet of fresh flowers and herbs balanced with fruit and crisp acidity. I fell in love instantly, and have championed the wine ever since.

In 2020, I came across a Dr. Konstantin Frank Rkastiteli 2006 in my cellar that I had forgotten about. A fourteen-year-old bottle of Rkatsiteli? Was I insane? I figured it would taste like sherry. I shrugged. At least I would open up some room in my overcrowded cellar. It was #openlocalwine Saturday, March 28, 2020. I had nothing to lose.

The wine was deep gold. A big whiff of honeydew, honeysuckle, dried apricots, and peach wafted out of the glass. There were also sherry-like notes. Dates. Nuts. It was all fruit up front, with a few semisweet/off-dry notes. It ended with a tremendous lemony kick that gave it terrific zip. The final result was a big mouthfeel wine, with lots of grip, layers, and structure.

Another great version of the wine is Blenheim Vineyards Rkatsiteli from Charlottesville, Virginia. Also from Virginia is the very drinkable Horton Vineyards Rkatsiteli. Other offerings to try are from Westport Rivers in Massachusetts, Whitewater Hill Vineyards in Grand Junction, Colorado, and Davesté Vineyards in North Carolina.

Perhaps most intriguing, Tomasello Winery, one of the largest wineries in New Jersey, makes a tasty sparkling Rkatsiteli, somewhat like a Prosecco, grown in the highly acclaimed Outer Coastal Plain, that I highly recommend.

Petit Manseng

Petit Manseng is a variety mostly grown in South West France. Here, you'll find it predominantly in California, Virginia, Georgia, and Ohio. This variety produces small, hardy berries. The resulting wine offers a nose of candied apples, peaches, and pineapple, as well as honey and abundant spice.

Virginia is the biggest producer in the United States. I have had a number of terrific Petit Mansengs, but a couple have made lasting impressions. Jeff White of Glen Manor Vineyards is among my favorite East Coast winemakers. I had written almost solely about his reds in the past. Petit Manseng is his smallest planting, only about 1.5 acres of the stuff, approximately 2,050 vines planted in 2008. Yet the Glen Manor Petit Manseng 2017 is one of their most memorable wines. Off-dry, it starts with candied notes of dried citrus, pineapple, and other tropical fruits. Slightly sweet, it is balanced with a lovely acidity that leaves a fresh and tingling feeling on the palate. Light, ethereal, and refreshing.

Other wonderful Petit Manseng offerings come from Linden Vineyards in the Blue Ridge Mountains, Early Mountain Vineyards (Madison County), Veritas Winery (Albemarle County), Horton Vineyards (Orange County), Fabbioli Cellars (Loudon County), Bluestone Vineyard (Shenandoah Valley), Pearmund Cellars (Fauquier County), Cana Vineyards (Loudoun County), and Michael Shaps Wineworks in Charlottesville.

Highly respected Ohio winemakers Joe and Kristi Juniper are making 100 percent estate-grown wines at Vermilion Valley Vineyards (Lake Erie Appellation), and they offer a slightly sweeter Petit Manseng. North

Carolina offers Jones von Drehle Petit Manseng. Sugarloaf Mountain Vineyard in Maryland also makes a very tasty version.

Roussanne

If you like Rhône whites, chances are you've had Roussanne, a classic French grape that hails from the Rhône. There it is usually blended with Marsanne. Roussanne is approved in the northern Rhône appellations of Crozes-Hermitage, Hermitage, and Saint-Joseph. It is also one of the grapes allowed in the southern Rhône appellation of Châteauneuf-du-Pape. In North America, Roussanne is planted in Canada (Okanagan Valley), California, Washington, Texas, Virginia, and New Jersey. Many wineries use it in blends, like Bonny Doon and Caymus. Varietal offerings, however, have become increasingly available over the past decade or so. Roussanne can be a big wine, very much like a Sauvignon Blanc or even a Chardonnay, depending on the winemaker. It is a terrific food wine that really shows off good cooking.

Tablas Creek Vineyard Roussanne Adelaida District Paso Robles is easily one of my favorites. They've been making it for the better part of two decades at their California winery. Aromatic and elegant, with notes of honeysuckle, apple, pear, oak, and pineapple. This is a big, rich wine that can stand up to chicken or pork, and spices. This was an eye-opening wine for me as far as Roussanne was concerned. Another terrific example is Truchard Vineyards Roussanne, also from California. The City Winery chain of tasting rooms offers Roussanne Reserve Cuvée Alder Springs, a delicious wine made with grapes from Mendocino.

Several wineries have planted Roussanne vines in Temecula, with lovely results, including Wilson Creek Winery Roussanne and Callaway Vineyard & Winery Roussanne.

Sonoma wineries tend to offer the classic version of this grape, pairing it with Marsanne. Corner 103 Marsanne Roussanne Sonoma Coast, Bartholomew Estate Marsanne | Roussanne Sonoma, and Cline Family Cellars Seven Ranchlands Marsanne Roussanne Sonoma Coast are all solid offerings of this traditional pairing. There are some lovely examples from the Santa Barbara region, including Epiphany Roussanne Camp Four Vineyard and Casa Dumetz Clementine Carter Roussanne.

Washington State also excels at this wine. Latta Wines, based in Seattle, produces a very pretty and drinkable version. Also impressive are the offerings from DeLille Cellars, Otis Kenyon Wine, and Maryhill Winery.

Just north of Washington, in the Okanagan Valley region of Canada, you'll find very good bottlings of Roussanne from Church & State Wines, Black Hills Estate Winery, and Terravista Vineyards.

There are versions in other areas as well, such as McPherson Roussanne Texas High Plains, and from Asheville, North Carolina, Biltmore Estate Limited Release Roussanne. Notable offerings from Virginia include Gabriele Rausse Winery Roussanne Redlands Vineyards, Michael Shaps Wineworks Roussanne, Blenheim Vineyards Roussanne, and Horton Vineyards Private Reserve Roussanne.

Sémillon

Sémillon is the other white grape backbone of the Bordeaux region. It is perhaps best known for being the grape that produces the best dessert wine in the world, Sauternes. Sémillon is considered an excellent blender grape, adding body, weight, and power to lighter wines.

To me, one of the best versions of this wine is L'Ecole No. 41 Columbia Valley Sémillon. I remember visiting during harvest, watching the cellar hands power washing the bins, press, destemmer, and machinery after that day's pick, with bright blue skies above, sipping the newest release of this exceptional wine. Aromatic, full, big, and chewy for a white, but made with finesse and elegance. Chateau Ste. Michelle Limited Release Sémillon is another good example from Washington State, as is the Sémillon from itä wines.

Birichino Sémillon Yount Mill Vineyard is an impressive California offering. Other standouts include Passaggio Sémillon, Newfound Wines Sémillon Yount Mill Vineyard, Kings Carey Sémillon, Osa Major Sierra Foothills Sémillon Gold In The Hills, and B.R.Cohn Sémillon North Coast.

Lock & Worth Sémillon from the Okanagan Valley in British Columbia is also quite enjoyable, as are Covert Farms Family Estate Sémillon and Tightrope Winery Sémillon from the same region.

Texas has some notable Sémillons from producers like Kerrville Hills Winery, Ron Yates Wines, and Brennan Vineyards. Spicewood Vineyards offers a sparkling Sémillon that is very much worth trying. In Colorado, Restoration Vineyards Sémillon is also very reliable.

Traminette

Around 1965, Herbert C. Barrett was a professor at the University of Illinois Urbana-Champaign. His work resulted in this new vine. Traminette is a result of crossbreeding the French American hybrid Joannes Seyve 23.416 and the German grape Gewürztraminer. The idea was to create a disease-resistant grape with greater cold hardiness that would give off the flavors and aromas of Gewürztraminer while being easier to grow. The wine has gained tremendous favor over the last decade or so. It is currently grown in Indiana, Ohio, the Yadkin Valley AVA of North Carolina, three of New York's four major growing regions (Niagara Escarpment, Finger Lakes, and Hudson Valley), Virginia, Pennsylvania, southern New England, and elsewhere.

New York offers several wonderful versions, chief among them being Fox Run Vineyards Traminette Simmons Vineyard, from the Finger Lakes. Truly elegant, it is off-dry, with a terrifically aromatic nose, a lovely, complex, and balanced wine that absolutely sings. Other fine examples include McGregor Vineyard Traminette, Goose Watch Dry Traminette, Thirsty Owl Wine Co. Traminette, Keuka Spring Vineyards Traminette, and Rooster Hill Vineyards Traminette. For a different spin, try Voleur Traminette Skin-Fermented, released through Montezuma Winery, an orange wine with a big nose and big flavors.

The Hudson Valley shows several nice bottlings from Benmarl Winery, Clearview Vineyard, Hudson-Chatham Winery, and Baldwin Vineyards. Whitecliff Vineyard Traminette shows off all the characteristics of this grape beautifully.

The very quaffable Rooftop Reds Traminette is made in Brooklyn. Johnson Estate Freelings Creek Reserve Sparkling Traminette, from the western part of the state, is a well-made sparkling version, perfect as a celebration wine.

Other examples abound—Working Dog Winery Estate Bottled Traminette, Bellview Winery Traminette Outer Coastal Plain, and Terhune Orchards Traminette are all from New Jersey. Black Birch Vineyard Traminette (Massachusetts) is very good. Benigna's Creek Winery, Stone Mountain Wine Cellars, Vynecrest Vineyards & Winery, Mazza Vineyards, and Cassel Vineyards of Hershey all offer good versions. Penns Woods Traminette is among the better ones in the state.

Two of the most elegant Traminettes in Michigan are St. Julian Winery Braganini Reserve Traminette Lake Michigan Shore and Detroit Vineyards Traminette. Other state producers include Fenn Valley Vineyards, Tanglewood Winery, Gravity Winery, and White Pine Winery, located on the shores of Lake Michigan.

Traminette is considered the state grape in Indiana. Huber Winery Traminette Knobstone Vineyard is a very good example. Other Indiana producers include Tonne Winery, French Lick Winery, Fruit Hills Winery, Heagy Vineyards, Butler Winery, Wildcat Creek Winery, and Easley Winery.

THIRTEEN OBSCURE RED GRAPES TO TRY

Like many others, I grew up on the classic reds. My parents drank Italian reds, Cabernet Sauvignon, Merlot, and Pinot Noir. Even today, these wines make for great treats, whether they are pulled from the cellar or a store shelf or a friend's collection.

On the other hand, I am a wine geek. I have been publishing, editing, and writing about wine for more than 25 years, and I have been making wine since 2006. It's important as a wine geek that I acknowledge for myself that wine is a food. You don't just drink it. You see it, you smell it, you swirl it, you savor it, you swish it around your mouth, you chew it, you swallow it. You don't do that with a glass of orange juice or a Diet Coke or water or coffee.

And despite being a massive creature of habit, I do not eat the same things all the time. As anyone, I have my favorites, but I like to live it up as well.

My first exposure to obscure grapes came when I visited the Hudson Valley Wine and Grape Growers Wine Competition. The entries were open to professional and amateur winemakers. I tasted Baco Noir, and fell in love. There were two that absolutely intrigued me. One was made by Benmarl Winery, which has been a big proponent of the grape going back to the 1960s. Its founder, Mark Miller, had appeared in *Time* magazine for his popular wines.

The other was made by an amateur (who, coincidentally, had worked at Benmarl in his youth), J. Stephen Casscles, whom I eventually became friends with. These Baco Noirs were somewhere between a Syrah and a Pinot Noir—as Steve would call them, "soft, approachable wines," with notes of sour cherry, cranberry, and brambleberry. I was so taken with them that we planted Baco Noir at our vineyard and began making wines from Steve's vineyard as well as our own. And we became famous for those wines at Hudson-Chatham, so much so that we became the first red wine made from hybrid grapes to get a score of 90 points or better from a major publication.

That began a crazy lust to try as many grapes as I could. I was very lucky, as Steve was a hybridizer, and had numerous experimental grapes named only with trial numbers. A hilarious ritual ensued. He'd show up at the farm, plunk down a dusty bottle, and we'd uncork it with a loaf of bread and some cheese. Crazy serial numbers were scrawled on masking tape or old labels. Steve would have me guess the parentage of the grape (at which I failed miserably). He would chatter on with all kinds of stories and information on each grape. As a home winemaker, Steve recycled any bottles he had for bottling his own small-production wines. I had him share some of these wines with writers. He never failed to bring something new, and even among the serial-numbered wines, I and others developed our own personal favorites.

The next such event was when Cameron Stark, former Robert Sinskey winemaker, then at Unionville Vineyards in New Jersey, introduced me to their estate Counoise. I was lucky enough to stop by on a drive home from a convention and caught a private barrel tasting with Cam and fellow winemaker Stephen "Zeke" Johnson. One whiff and, again, I was in love. Rewards like this fuel my desire to try something new and keep an open mind.

Here's a list of some of these obscure red wine grapes you should try. Are they easy to come by? Not always. But isn't that part of the fun?

Baco Noir

This variety was developed by Monsieur François Baco of France during the great phylloxera epidemic that wiped out many of the country's vineyards. He crossbred numerous plants, looking for a vine with tough roots (impervious to the vine louse) that would produce good fruit and make great wine. Heron Hill Winery in New York's Finger Lakes region and Henry of Pelham Family Estate Winery in Canada's Niagara region both make a lighter-styled Baco Noir, more akin to a Pinot Noir/Syrah blend. Girardet Vineyards of Roseburg, Oregon, makes a bigger, bolder, chewy Baco Noir.

Blaufränkisch

This red wine emanates from Central Europe, growing in Austria, the Czech Republic, Germany, Slovakia, Croatia, Serbia, Slovenia, Hungary, and Italy. It is known by several names, including Lemberger in the United States, where it is particularly popular in Pennsylvania, Washington State, Michigan, New Jersey, Idaho, New York, Colorado, Ohio, Virginia, and California. There are many good Blaufränkisch wines in the US. Four of my favorites come from Beneduce Vineyards (New Jersey), Red Tail Ridge Winery (New York's Finger Lakes), Johan Vineyards (Willamette Valley, Oregon), and Vermilion Valley Vineyards in Ohio (theirs is listed as Lemberger).

Chambourcin

Chambourcin is a variety that has been around since 1963, bred from grapes that hark back to the 1860s. It's a versatile grape, great for rosé wines, dry red wines (where it does require, like Zinfandel, some good oak aging), and Port (due to its deep fruit and high acidity). The grape is grown across the country, and produces a big, purply red wine that features black cherry, plum, and some herbaceous notes. William Heritage Burn Pile Vineyard Estate Grown Chambourcin from New Jersey's renowned Outer Coastal Plain and Port of Leonardtown Winery Chambourcin Reserve from Maryland are among my favorites.

Cinsault

I found a bottle of Turley Wine Cellars Cinsault largely by accident. I was looking for their Zinfandel, and pulled a bottle of Cinsault instead. I fell in love instantly, and would pour the wine for wine writers who stopped by our farm in Upstate New York, until my supply ran out. Cinsault (which can also be spelled Cinsaut) is one of the grapes used in Rhône blends and Provençal rosés. It exhibits gorgeous ripe cherry as well as hints of brambleberry, red cassis, and dried cranberries. It has a well-deserved fandom around the world and is widely grown in South Africa, where it produces exceptional wines, as well as in other parts of Africa, Australia, Italy, and the US.

Without question, my favorite Cinsault is Turley Bechthold Vineyard Cinsault. Planted in 1886, this Lodi, California, vineyard is the oldest in the country. And it shows. The fruit is bright and in your face, but the middle is all berry and spice, and the finish is fresh fruit.

I have two favorites from Temecula: Leoness Cellars Tucalota Vineyard, which is impressive, and Longshadow Ranch Cinsault, an absolute capper—complex, layered, balanced. Both are keepers from this small, fun region.

In Texas, where Cinsault is very well-known, it is as popular as a rosé but also does double duty making great red wines. William Chris Vineyards Cinsault Lost Draw Vineyards Texas High Plains is an absolute keeper! Colorado's Buckel Family Wine Cinsault is another shocker to look out for. Joe and Shamai Buckel's wine explodes with bright cherries and fresh strawberries, with a hint of spice.

Gamay Noir

Gamay Noir (often referred to as just Gamay) is famous for being the featured grape of Beaujolais, but it is grown across the United States and Canada. There are some exceptional versions of this wine. One of my absolute favorites is from Tawse Winery in the Niagara Bench region of Canada. Their Gamay is light, fruity, and delicate. From the same region, I also like the Gamay Noir of 13th Street Winery. Next up would be Thomas Houseman's Anne Amie Vineyards Gamay Noir, from the winery's Twelve Oaks Estate vineyard in the Chehalem Mountains AVA in Oregon. And there are also two to try from New York State: Sheldrake Point Winery Gamay Noir and Whitecliff Vineyard Gamay Noir, both extremely light and elegant.

Lagrein

Lagrein is a grape from the northern Italian Alps, in the South Tyrol. It is native to the Alto Adige region, and the Italians make many great wines with it. The grape is now grown in Australia and the United States, largely in the Central Coast AVA (California) and Umpqua Valley AVA (Oregon). But there are also a few acres being grown here and there across the country. *New York Times* wine journalist Eric Asimov wrote of Lagrein that is produces "congenial, straightforward wines that can be deliciously plummy, earthy and chewy, dark and full-bodied but not heavy, with a pronounced minerally edge." I first encountered the wine at Red

Tail Ridge Winery, tasting Nancy Irelan's fantastic wine. Christopher Tracy makes a supremely quaffable version of this wine at Channing Daughters Winery on Long Island. Oregon's Remy Wines Estate Lagrein is an exceptional version made by iconic winemaker Remy Drabkin. Another favorite, from California's Central Coast, is Pelletiere Estate Riserva Lagrein from the Paso Robles Willow Creek District, which has a long track record of producing highly acclaimed Lagrein in the US. Also from Paso Robles is Tobin James Silver Reserve Lagrein, which is also highly commendable.

Mourvèdre

Mourvèdre is best known in the Rhône and Provence regions of France but is also grown in Spain (known as Monastrell), Australia, and South Africa, as well California, Washington, Texas, and elsewhere in the US. Mourvèdre produces big red wines with dark berry flavors and some earthy notes. William Chris Vineyards Lost Draw Vineyards Mourvèdre from Texas is one of the best there is. Soft, full, and impressive, with hints of cranberry, cherry, and spice. Leoness Cellars Mourvèdre, from Temecula, California, is an absolute revelation. Big, lovely fruit, filled with plum, prune, cherry, and spice. It's a wine of exceptional finesse. The Meeker Vineyard Mourvèdre La Sierra Vineyard Lake County is also excellent. Chateau Ste. Michelle Limited Release Mourvèdre from Washington contains a touch of Syrah and is aged in French and American oak. Lovely and impressive.

Norton

Norton is one of the most famous of the obscure grapes, having been featured by Todd Kliman in his best-selling book *The Wild Vine: A Forgotten Grape and the Untold Story of American Wine*. In it, Kliman explains how Norton made a name for American wine in Missouri a hundred years before California put American wines on the map in the 1970s. Named for Dr. Daniel Norton, the grape was first cultivated in Virginia in the 1820s and became commercially available in the 1830s, before migrating to Missouri, where it won a host of medals. Because of this history, some grape historians consider Norton the quintessential American grape. It then seemingly disappeared before being brought back into vogue, and is now grown in a number of states, including Missouri, Ohio, and Virginia. It is a fantastic pairing with game and pasta dishes.

The grape produces a dark purple wine, with flavors of blackberry, dark raspberry, blueberry, and cassis, with a hefty note of spice. Stone Hill Winery was established in 1847, in Hermann, Missouri, and found acclaim when their Norton wine was named "Best Wine of All Nations" at the 1879 Vienna World Exposition. Stone Hill Old Vine Reserve Norton is one of the best produced in the country. This small-batch release is made from the fruit of vines planted before the Civil War. It is hard to come by but well worth the effort. Big, intense, rich, and cellar worthy, this wine never fails to impress.

Dennis Horton is credited with reintroducing Norton in Virginia in 1992 at his Horton Vineyards. It was the first Norton varietal wine commercially produced in Virginia since Prohibition. Over the next twenty years, the grape rose from an obscure oddity to cult status. Horton Vineyards Norton is a deep purple wine, with big notes of plum and cherry on the nose and palate. Another winner from Virginia is DuCard Vineyards Norton, which is big, complex, and well-balanced.

Petit Verdot

Petit Verdot has, for centuries, been one of the grapes used by the great Bordeaux houses in their blends. It is a big, dark grape that makes an inky purple wine featuring lots of dark fruit and high acidity. It's a great blender, to be sure, adding depth and flavor to many wines. The varietal wine can be super deep and intense, with supple tannins and a velvety quality that's hard to explain. Those who like it are big, big fans. Count me in!

Among all the Petit Verdot wines out there, I like Richard Olsen-Harbich's Bedell Cellars Petit Verdot, from the North Fork of Long Island. It is big, rich, fruity, and supple, with a smooth finish and some nice spice. A gorgeous wine coaxed along by the maritime climate of Long Island and one of the East Coast's best winemakers. New Jersey has two good versions, Palmaris Reserve Petit Verdot from Tomasello Winery and OA Petit Verdot from Hawk Haven Vineyard & Winery.

Walla Walla Valley in Washington State is the home of Reininger Winery, which makes the exceptional Reininger Helix Petit Verdot. It is 100 percent PV aged in 100 percent French oak (30 percent in new oak). Sweet dark plum and spicy tobacco. Notes of pomegranate and cranberry. On the palate are blackberry, marionberry, dark raspberry, and red cherry. A lingering smoky finish.

Another wonderful bottling is that of Veritas Winery of Virginia. This is a more classic version of the wine. Big and deep, with stewed blackberry and lekvar, cassis, and other soft notes. Silky and powerful. I also like Paradise Springs Petit Verdot. This is a unique version, brighter and fresher than other offerings of this wine. Big floral notes on the nose and lots of raspberry and blackberry, with hints of cassis. Something really different.

Tempranillo

Is there another grape as versatile and elegant as Tempranillo? It is the backbone of the wines of Rioja, although it is grown throughout Spain and Portugal. It became so popular that it was named one of the top five grown grapes in the world, yet few people really know about the actual grape, since most Spanish wines are named for the house and not the grape.

"To get elegance and acidity out of Tempranillo, you need a cool climate. But to get high sugar levels and the thick skins that give deep color you need heat. In Spain these two opposites are best reconciled," wrote the wine writer and my friend Oz Clarke.

I found one of my favorite plantings of this grape while traveling the West Coast at Abacela, in Roseburg, in the Umpqua Valley of Southern Oregon. Their Tempranillo Estate Barrel Select is aged in French (97 percent) and American (3 percent) oak (9 percent new, 18 percent two years old, 73 percent neutral oak). This is Abacela's flagship Tempranillo. Rich blackberry, black currant with hints of blue fruits, violets, mocha, and spice. Beautiful structure. Nice tannins. Super velvety. And a long, long finish.

Another magical Tempranillo comes from a small estate winery in Napa Valley. Chris Madrigal (whose family has been farming in Napa for three generations) runs one of the best artisanal wineries in the region. The Madrigal Family Winery Tempranillo is a reserva Rioja-styled Tempranillo. Big, rich, with dark and red fruits and a nice touch of oak.

Vino Salida Tempranillo from Grand Valley, in Poncha Springs, Colorado, is another one to try. This highly acclaimed small-production wine has won numerous awards.

Tannat

I had my first Tannat from Doug Fabbioli of Fabbioli Cellars, in Loudon County, Virginia. A friend, wine connoisseur David Jackson, had brought over a bottle to share. Historically Tannat has been cultivated in South West France in the Madiran AOC. It is also grown in Australia, South Africa, and South America, where it is considered the "national grape" of Uruguay but is also grown in Argentina, Peru, Brazil, and Bolivia. In the United States, Tannat is grown in Maryland, Virginia, California, Arizona, Oregon, and Texas. It makes a big, deep, rich wine, dark in color and flavor. Doug Fabbioli's Tannat is a beautifully balanced and complex wine, with dark, dark fruits like blackberry, black cherry, lekvar, and cassis.

Another unforgettable version is William Chris Vineyards Hye Estate Vineyard Tannat. The color is dark, with notes of dark stewed fruits, leather, and spice. Big and chewy, balanced and elegant.

Michael Shaps Tannat is another well-made, super-fun-to-drink red wine, from the Monticello region of Virginia. Barrel aged for eighteen months, it is full of dark stewed fruit and spice, with big tannins and acidity. A chewy mouthful.

Teroldego

Teroldego is an Italian cultivar that is related to such grapes as Marzemino, Lagrein, and Syrah. Teroldego is mostly grown in Italy, in particular the northeastern region of Trentino-Alto Adige/Südtirol. The grape makes a big, spicy wine dark and robust. In the last ten years, plantings of this grape in California have shot up dramatically.

The first varietal wine I had of this was from Nancy Irelan's Red Tail Ridge Winery, located on the western shore of Seneca Lake in the Finger Lakes region. The former Gallo winemaker, along with her husband, vineyard manager Mike Schnelle, makes an absolutely stunning version as part of their Red Tail Ridge Obscure Red Varietal Series. It is big and rich and super flavorful. On occasion, they have offered a sparkling version of this wine as well.

Wilson Creek Winery in Temecula, California, offers a very drinkable version of this wine. Boasting big purple fruit with chewy tannins and lovely acidity, this wine lingers for a long time.

LangeTwins Family Winery in Acampo offers their Single Barrel The Eighty Vineyard Teroldego as their premium version of this varietal wine. These grapes are grown at Jahant Woods 02 Vineyard in the Jahant AVA. Dark cherry and blueberry notes are offset by spice and pine and a certain nuttiness. Complex and impressive.

Zweigelt

The Zweigelt is a relatively new grape, developed in Austria in 1922 by Friedrich Zweigelt (1888–1964). The grape is a cross between St. Laurent and Blaufränkisch, and has found favor in Austria, Hungary, Slovakia, the Czech Republic, and New Zealand. In America, it is grown in Washington, New York, and other states. It is a great cool-climate grape. The resulting wines tend to be light to medium bodied, with fresh fruitiness up front and nice, zippy acidity on the end. These are great lunch wines and wonderful with lighter fare.

Goose Watch Zweigelt Finger Lakes (with 12 percent Marquette) is a lovely example of what this varietal wine can be. As Lenn Thompson of Cork Report Media wrote, this wine "smells of bright, fresh strawberries and raspberries with subtle hints of vanilla and oak-born spice. That vanilla character is a bit more forward on a juicy, medium-bodied palate driven by ripe, intense red raspberry fruit flavor, along with background notes of strawberry and savory spice. The acidity is fresh, and I think this is a wine that would work well with a light chill in the summer." That's why you need to try Zweigelt.

I am a huge fan of Lailey Winery from the Niagara River VQA in Canada. Their Zweigelt is an exceptional version of this wine. A single vineyard wine, fermented in small lots, with a little less than a year in neutral barrels, results in an incredibly delicate light red wine, with fresh red fruit up front and perfect acidity. This wine lingers on the palate.

Johan Vineyards, in the newly established Van Duzer Corridor AVA in Oregon, is known for their biodynamic farming and irreverent attitude. But they are serious about making wine. Their Zweigelt is filled with bright fruit, a certain earthiness, and a wallop of spice. Fruity but dry, this zippy red wine has garnered a small cult following that continues to grow.

Keuka Spring Zweigelt Traditional Method Sparkling from the Finger Lakes is a beautiful pink and explodes with strawberry for a little something different.

There are, of course, other grapes—too many to mention. The point is, you should always leap at the chance to try a new grape. What do you have to lose? The more you try, the more you understand about the world of wine, and about yourself.

MARQUETTE WINE

No grape in recent memory has so irrevocably changed the American winemaking landscape as Marquette. "The Marquette wine grape was released in 2006 by the University of Minnesota breeding program and shortly thereafter nursery orders were being filled for shipment in northern states from Minnesota to Maine," wrote New England wine expert Todd Trzaskos for the *New York Cork Report*.

The genius behind the grape breeding program at UM was Elmer Swenson, who owned a 120-acre farm near Osceola, Minnesota. He first started breeding grapes in 1943, and from 1969 to 1979, he husbanded fruit crops at the University of Minnesota. The university began its grape breeding program in the mid-1970s, with his impetus. The idea was to develop cold-hardy grape varieties suitable for making red wine that would have good depth of color, flavor, and balance between tannins and acidity. These grapes would need to be able to weather harsh winters, bud late in the spring (to avoid hard-frost events), and ripen before the first fall frost. Given that this was aimed at cold-climate locales, the fruit needed to ripen in an extremely short window, as such places usually had short summers.

Other grapes that were developed as part of this program include Frontenac, Frontenac Gris, La Crescent, Edelweiss, and Itasca. Also, Swenson additionally conducted work at his own farm, developing his own varieties, which are similarly cold hardy and include St. Cross, St. Pepin, Prairie Star, and Briana. But the star of the program has been Marquette, which, in addition to ticking all the boxes for cold hardiness, color, flavor, and balance, according to the University of Minnesota, has "moderate resistance to black rot, botrytis bunch rot, downy mildew and powdery mildew."

"A rigorous hand breeding program produced this vine and years of field trials led to its selection for release. Marquette's parentage is oft touted because of its hip and revered grandparent pinot noir," Trzaskos wrote in his article. "However, also take notice of the other side of the family, where a certain wild riparia #64 got involved with great-grandparent Carmine, a Californian sprout that is the child of great-great grandparents merlot and cabernet sauvignon." In short, the parentage of this grape gave farmers and winemakers in northern climates great hope. Many farmers signed on for trials that began in the early 2000s.

I first started tasting Marquette when the initial wines released around 2010 or so, mostly coming out of Minnesota, made by university professors. The wine was adequate, but not super impressive. However, in 2012, my socks were knocked off by the wine produced at Lincoln Peak Vineyard in Vermont. Co-owners Chris and Michaela Granstrom began planting cold-hardy grapevines in 2001. In 2012, Chris (who is also the winemaker) took me in the barrel room, where we tasted the 2011 Marquette. Bright cassis, raspberry, and blackberry all greeted me on the nose and on the palate. A touch of black pepper on the back end.

In 2015, Granstrom brought with him to the Eastern Wineries Exposition several bottles of his newest, Lincoln Peak Marquette 2013. People flocked from around the large ballroom to get a taste of this wine. Throughout the exposition, you would hear people inquiring, "Did you taste the Lincoln Peak Marquette yet?" It drew that kind of attention. At the winery, limits were put on how many bottles could be purchased, and it became a cult wine.

That vintage clocked in at 14 percent alcohol and had a deeper color than the previous vintages. It was clearly a much bigger wine. The earlier vintages tasted like Pinot Noir or at least had a Rhône-ish character. This newest vintage was a whole new animal, and it not only advanced Marquette's stature, but that of East Coast winemaking. This was a

California-styled wine that was grown, estate made, and bottled entirely in Vermont. But it tasted like California. The Marquette 2013 had more in common with a Turley Zinfandel or a big Syrah than it did with any East Coast wine. Hugely concentrated, it exploded with plum, cassis, even prune, with lovely, silky tannins, great layers of flavors and complexity, and a fantastic finish. It was easily the best Marquette I had tasted up to that point.

In 2016, Marquette impressed a large corps of wine writers from Canada to Virginia as they gathered for the TasteCamp 2016: Vermont, organized by writers Lenn Thompson and Todd Trzaskos. The Granstroms' Marquette was impressive, as usual. At the same time, Ethan Joseph, winemaker of neighboring Shelburne Vineyard, wowed the crowd with his unoaked Marquette. Joseph was a young, passionate rising star, and his pouring of that wine reinforced what the writers were already suspecting—Marquette was a game-changer.

"About two dozen new vineyards have started up in the last seven or eight years because of the availability of these new grapes," Gerry Barnhart of Victory View Vineyard, near Saratoga Springs in the Upper Hudson Valley, told Eric Asimov of *The New York Times*. "Before, you couldn't even think about growing wine grapes here."

A movement began. Symposiums arose, focused solely on cold-climate grape growing. The Northern Grapes Project ran from 2011 to 2016, funded by the U.S. Department of Agriculture. "The emergence of cold hardy, *Vitis riparia*–based wine grape cultivars in the 1990s created a new and rapidly expanding industry of small vineyard and winery enterprises in more than 12 states in New England, northern New York, and the Upper Midwest, boosting rural economies in those regions," touted the organization's website. It also helped spawn the International Cool Climate Wine Symposium, which meets every four years in different cities around the world.

Marquette can be found in many states these days and is becoming more and more a staple of wine production throughout the country. It is in the hands of many small craft producers. But wine consumers are increasingly conscious of the new grape and, more importantly, are advocates and fans. This is definitely a grape you should be aware of.

Shelburne Vineyard

Ethan Joseph has made a name for himself as the winemaker at Shelburne Vineyard in Shelburne, Vermont. He started there early in 2008, and became obsessed with the science, art, and mystery of wine. He was also fortunate enough to have the full support of Shelburne's owners, Ken and Gail Albert. With this kind of backing, and passion, Ethan is now counted among the best winemakers in New England and on the East Coast.

Shelburne Vineyard now manages the old Lincoln Peak vineyards (with Granstrom still involved and the wines sold under the Iapetus brand). They have also joined forces with Eden Ciders. Eden founder, Eleanor Léger (a titan of the cider industry), is the CEO of the new combined companies.

Iapetus Subduction Marquette is made with the majority of the grapes destemmed and left uncrushed, with 10 percent whole clusters. The grapes are left on the skins for 86 days, then pressed and placed in barrels within 24 hours. The wine generally ages sur lie (in contact with the lees) in barrels of various ages for approximately eight months. Joseph performs bâtonnage weekly, stirring the lees back into the wine. The whole berries and carbonic maceration lend a fruitiness to the wine. Medium cherries, raspberries, and plum come across. It's soft and lush, with lovely layers. Ends with leather and black pepper, and the fruit lingers a nice, long time. This is a sexy, sultry red wine, classy and sophisticated.

Victory View Vineyard

I became a fan of Victory View Vineyard early on. Gerry Barnhart and his wife, Mary, have been making great wines in the cold Upper Hudson Valley, above Albany, since 2012 (they first planted in 2008). Their Marquette vines are farmed with care, and the wine is handmade, aged in oak. Barnhart relies on malolactic fermentation to soften the wine, reducing the acidity. The winery won medals and praise galore with their first two vintages and have never looked back. "Connoisseurs might not be ready to rank these cold-weather wines among European classics, but cold-hardy varieties are quickly gaining recognition," wrote Eric Asimov in *The New York Times* in an article featuring Victory View and Marquette. Victory View Independence Marquette is a big, Syrah-like wine, with plum, cassis, and cherry and hints of pepper and vanilla.

Wild Arc Farm

Winemaker Todd Cavallo made a very impressive Marquette in 2020 that scored 91 points from *Wine Enthusiast*. Made in the shadow of the Shawangunks on the west wide of the Hudson River, it was a major fruit bomb, featuring violets, blueberries, and tobacco along with cherries and spice. A super-impressive wine of flavor and depth from one of the East Coast's most influential natural garagistes.

La Garagista Farm + Winery

La Garagista is on Mount Hunger, not far from Bethel, Vermont, and was founded in 1999 by the husband-and-wife team of Deirdre Heekin and Caleb Barber. Deirdre is the winegrower, organizer, writer, photographer, flower farmer, and designer. Caleb is the gardener, chef extraordinaire, designer, builder, mechanic, factotum, philosopher, and farm manager.

Their work at the farm and winery, both in the field and in the cellar, is guided by regenerative, permaculture, and biodynamic practices.

Their land has been farmed for more than two hundred years. It is in four separate parcels: two adjacent vineyards separated by a seasonal country road, and two others in the nearby Champlain Valley. Their mission is to make quality wines and ciders that express their terroir and their individual vintages. La Garagista makes natural wines and ciders as hands-off as possible.

If you're a wine geek, or just enjoy wine casually, you will love La Garagista. The fruit is handpicked and sorted, foot crushed, and made in small lots. They rely on wild yeast and use little to no sulfites at bottling—whether or how much they use depends on the wine and the season. Their tasting room is in their barn.

La Garagista In A Dark Country Sky is made from Marquette estate grown on clay and limestone. The wine is fermented whole cluster with wild yeast. It is a bright, fruity, spicy, medium-bodied red. Young and vibrant, with good, mouthwatering acidity. No sulfites. You might like it chilled, Deirdre and Caleb suggest, but I enjoy it at room temperature, with lunch or with a dinner of roast chicken or pork.

Elmaro Vineyard

Elmaro Vineyard, located in Wisconsin, features a white pine on their labels. The site of the vineyard was homesteaded in the 1850s, and that pine tree, estimated to be about 300 years old, still sits on the property.

Elmaro is family owned and run, having planted their first vines in 2006. Mark Delaney has farmed this place since he was a boy. Mark sold almost every piece of farming equipment he owned in 2010 and turned it over to start a winery. He said, "I accomplished my dream of farming. It's time to help someone else achieve theirs."

Elmaro Marquette is aged in American and French oak for two years. It is a medium-bodied red with notes of fresh cherries and raspberries, lots of plum, and a hint of vanilla. The wine is complex, well-balanced, and incredibly drinkable.

Burr Vineyards

Located in the town of Brandon in the Lakes Region in central Minnesota, Burr Vineyards is a family-owned boutique winery. The Ledermann family has been growing grapes on this 95-acre farm since 1999. Overlooking Burr Lake, the Ledermanns grow fourteen varieties of cold-hardy grapes. Founder and winemaker Florian Ledermann leads the winemaking team. Katie Ledermann and her husband, Peter, became partners in the business in 2019. Burr Vineyards Marquette Estate Grown (Black Label) is a lovely, fruit-forward wine with hints of plum and cherry, and notes of spice and cocoa.

Jomas Hill Vineyard

Tom and Joyce Carlson own Jomas Hill Vineyard, located in Darwin, Minnesota. Tom has farmed his entire life, and converted his dairy farm to a vineyard. Marquette was planted in 2009. Jomas Hill Marquette Reserve is made from estate grapes that were pressed, fermented, and aged in barrels. The wine is redolent of juicy black cherry, and has good tannins, a note of vanilla, and a nice peppery finish.

Petoskey Farms Vineyard & Winery

"Many of the best Marquette-based wines I've tasted have come from the Northeast," noted wine writer Lenn Thompson. "This Michigan-grown example from Petoskey Farms Vineyard & Winery…is an exception to that rule." Owned by Andy and Tracie Roush, the winery has produced a string of impressive vintages. Petoskey Farms Marquette Top of the Mitt is one of the best Marquette wines in the country. Dark cherry, stewed strawberries, and cocoa lead off this dark red, medium-bodied wine. There's tobacco, leather, and black pepper. Lovely tannins and a long finish.

Redside Ranch Vineyard

Redside Ranch is a family-run operation in the Deschutes and Lower Bridge area of Central Oregon. They partnered with Elixir Wine Group, a wine importer, in 2011, to make wines for the Elixir portfolio. Elixir's internationally known winemaker, Christopher Kirk Ermisch, created the wine. The 2019 Redside Ranch Marquette was their first vintage, and it won gold at the prestigious *San Francisco Chronicle* wine competition. "Redside Ranch Vineyard Manager Kerry Damon has been a tireless advocate of growing cold hardy, French/American hybrid grapes in Central Oregon. Their Marquette was a pleasure to make, it was hand-picked and tasted delicious right off the vine," said Ermisch in a press release at the time of the win.

Many on the West Coast stood up and took notice.

Georgian Hills Vineyards

Winemaker Ky Tynan has made a supple wine in the Blue Mountains of Ontario, Canada. The original founding partners, John Ardiel, a fourth-generation apple grower, and Robert Ketchin, with forty-plus years of experience in the wine business, made this a formidable winery that has gained much attention for their quality work.

Georgian Hills Vineyards Marquette is "a truly enjoyable example of Marquette, showing the enormous potential for quality wines from this grape," wrote Jamie Drummond for *Good Food Revolution*, calling it "a terrific Ontario Marquette." It leads off with the smell of blackberry and blueberry cobbler. The palate has notes of plum and spice, and plenty of black pepper. There's an excellent balance of tannins and acidity, and the flavor lingers a long time.

ROSÉ

One of my favorite memories of rosé harkens back to a small bend in the Ebro River, in Spain, in the vineyards of Bodegas Muga in 2011. Bodegas Muga was founded by Isaac Muga and Aurora Caño in 1932. Winemaker Jorge Muga was entertaining us. He threw a half dozen bunches of bound vineyard cuttings on the ground and set fire to them. He then took some sausages, clamped them in a camper's grill, and tossed it on the fire. Next he split open several Spanish baguettes, laid the freshly grilled sausages on the bread, and passed them around.

For the wine, he chose a rosé from his current vintage from the tank. Bodegas Muga Rosado is made from a blend of about 60 percent Garnacha, 30 percent Viura, and 10 percent Tempranillo. He had stored some wine for us in a decanter with a small pouring arm. With no glasses, each of us had to pour the wine directly into our mouths. We took turns holding the oddly shaped decanter, spilling the wine into our waiting mouths—and over our chins—as the river flowed by. Fresh flavors of strawberry, cherry, and tropical fruits were powered home by a fresh acidity.

I complimented Jorge on the sausages, which were remarkably flavorful. I asked him where he had gotten them. He laughed. "I made it," he said proudly. Did he raise pigs? No, he shook his head, "I shot one son of bitch over there," pointing to a part of the vineyard. "A wild boar. And I shot another over there. Venison." I will never forget the freshness of the sandwich, how perfectly the wine matched its spiciness, and how it all went together so beautifully.

My own relationship with rosé is a complicated one. I have sipped rosé, quaffed rosé, made rosé in any number of ways. One of my most recent experiences was the tasting of East Coast rosés in March 2022 with Lenn Thompson, author of the *Cork Report* newsletter and owner of Cork Report Media. Lenn and I have been friends since we first started blogging about wine back in the mid-2000s. Today, Lenn is among the top reviewers of East Coast wines. The event was an open-invitation blind tasting of more than forty rosé wines from the eastern half of the United States. Submissions included wines from Maryland, Michigan, New Jersey, New York, Ohio, Pennsylvania, Virginia, and Wisconsin.

It was a unique experience, particularly when one considers that 82 percent of all the rosé imported into the United States in the early 1980s was from Portugal—mostly Mateus, which was established in 1942, and became popular in the UK during the 1950s. By the 1960s and 1970s it had become a hit in the US. The wine itself accounted for 40 percent of Portugal's overall wine exports. For many years, this was the dominant rosé in America. Today, Mateus is no longer the industry titan it was, and rosé as a category has risen meteorically since the turn of the century. It went from an occasional wine, somewhat seasonal, to a staple that holds its own sizable space now.

Also participating as a taster at this event was Gibson Campbell, wholesale sales director of Macari Vineyards, of New York's North Fork region, and a former writer for the *New York Cork Report*. I knew Gibson very well, and we had tasted together many times at professional tastings and in social settings, in living rooms, kitchens, and patios, with other wine friends.

The three of us tasted through the wines together, blind, and starred the ones we thought were worthy of tasting again. We came back to the starred wines, and retasted. Eventually, we tore off the paper coverings to reveal the wines we liked. We started around 10 a.m. and went into the late afternoon. We took care to enjoy the wines, but to mark them carefully.

Gibson told us what he looked for in a rosé. "When I'm drinking or shopping for rosé, I'm typically looking for three main attributes: acid structure, ample fruit, and an overall completeness in the wine. Acid is kind of a no-brainer. It has to have enough zip and malic acid to make the wine feel alive and refreshing. Without it, there's really no reason to drink it."

He looked for wines that are "lithe and delicate but have generous fruit flavors as well. Sure, some citrus is great, but I love when a winemaker pushes the ripeness a bit, and you end up with more ripe orchard fruit like white peach and fresh apricot to round out the palate." And when he considered "completeness," "It's almost like looking for complexity in red wine. I'm not expecting layers upon layers of fruit, but I want the wine to feel like it's not missing anything."

For Lenn Thompson, "My personal floor for rosé is maybe a bit lower than it is for other styles or individual varieties. The things I want with rosé are pretty simple: freshness, fruit, and then one more 'something else.' I like rosés that strike a balance between fruity and savory qualities, but that 'something else' can also take the form of floral, mineral, or spice components. I don't expect a ton of complexity with rosé, but when I find acidity, great fruit, and then one other thing, I get excited about that wine." I quite agree.

On the East Coast, a lot of the classic rosé is made from Cabernet Franc. It has the trinity of cherry, strawberry, and creamy lime finish that so many people expect from a rosé. Many are done in that soft Provençal style.

As I grew up, wine was an important part of the meal. Weekend lunches, as I began college, were often consumed with rosé. Getting older, I began drinking rosé from France and rosato from Italy, and a few from Spain. So, I had a very European view of rosé. But over time I found some of the less traditional rosés even more compelling.

In this tasting it was the nontraditional wines that stood out. The Provençal-styled rosés were lovely, but the ones I wanted to keep drinking were the more individualistic ones. Additionally, I really liked Lenn's take when he wrote, "I'm publishing this report in the summer—smack dab in the middle of 'rosé season,' but I don't consider rosé to be seasonal. Yes, some wineries and wine marketers have beer-ified rosé, trying to make it seasonal, but I'm not buying it."

He was absolutely right, of course. Rosé is a great year-round wine, wonderful with lunches, light fare, even things like roast chicken, roast pork, and seafood. A well-made rosé is always the right answer, no matter the time of year.

Rosé vs. Blush:
What's the Difference?

Generally speaking, rosé is a dry pink wine, blush is sweet pink wine. It's pretty simple.

Rosé tends to be a more serious wine. At quality houses, it is made with great care, and usually has some sort of ethos behind it, like most serious winemaking. On the other hand, there are no hard-and-fast rules where blush is concerned. That doesn't mean blush is bad wine. Blush is probably the most popular wine in America—think White Zinfandel. A good blush wine has a decent amount of sugar, but not to the point of becoming cloying, with the acidity balancing it out.

Winemaker Bob Trinchero made the first White Zinfandel in 1972. He bled off a certain amount of free-run juice while making his Amador County Zinfandel. The idea was to make the remaining juice darker by separating out the lighter early juice. This is the classic French method for making a rosé. The resulting wine became popular. Three years later, a slightly sweeter version became a major hit, and an entire category was born. Sweet pink wines make up a large portion of California's annual production.

Dating back to the 1940s and 1950s, New York State's Finger Lakes region had already had a major hit with what wine industry folks called "Pink Cats," rose-hued wines made from the Catawba grape. The Catawba grape has pink flesh. When pressed, the juice is already pink. These wines are sweet, and have remained a popular staple, despite the rise of world world-class in the region.

ROSÉ 101

There are three ways to make rosé wine. Two are very specific to the history of rosé winemaking. The other is a commercial endeavor, but produces fine wines nonetheless.

There are no rules in the world of rosé. Rosé is an enological meritocracy. Winemakers can use any grape they want to make an excellent rosé. Anyone who says otherwise is a buffoon.

The saignée method is the most traditional. Saignée means "to bleed." The idea is to press red grapes, to take the first-run juice, which is usually the lightest, and to bleed that wine off from the rest of the red wine. As the press pushes harder to extract the juice, the colors tend to darken. Thus, two things are achieved. The winemaker creates a darker, deeper red, and gets another wine out of the same grapes. Oftentimes, these are the best wines in the category.

Lenn Thompson refers to the next method as "rosé on purpose." In this case, a winemaker presses red grapes with the idea of making only rosé wine, usually picking them before normal red ripeness, when the grapes show a high acidity and some solid vestiges of light cherry, strawberry, and other bright red fruits. Often the grapes are crushed, destemmed, and allowed to steep for 24 to 48 hours (and some much, much less), and then immediately pressed. This results in a pink wine with lovely color, acidity, and flavor.

When a new vineyard block is planted, the third-year fruit is harvested early so that the vines have time to recover and harden over properly to better survive a cold winter. Also, some vineyards are planted in less-than-advantageous spots (sometimes on purpose, sometimes not), and the grapes may never ripen fully. These vineyards can provide rosé wines for many years and fulfill a need the winery has for product.

The third method is blending. I have had many lovely wines where a white wine (or a blend of white wines) is tinged by the addition of a red wine. The best of these are very much thought out ahead of time, and can result in impressive wines, particularly fragrant whites combined with a touch of a fruity red.

As a winemaker, I have used all three methods, and I prefer the saignée method. There is nothing finer than sitting on the press deck in the early morning, tasting the free run as it comes off the press. The best ones taste like strawberry wine. Those are glorious harvest mornings, with the sky blue, a slight chill in the air, and the smell wafting up through the press deck as the staff hurries the grapes through their process. You raise a small glass of fresh, hazy juice amongst the staff, and everyone's eyes light up.

CLASSIC FRENCH ROSÉS

The classic French rosé that I and other wine folks aspire to is Bandol Tempier rosé. Bandol is a seaside town on the Côte d'Azur near the city of Toulon. It has a reputation for producing the finest rosés in the world. Bandol Tempier rosé is made with 50 percent Mourvèdre; the remainder is part Grenache and part Cinsault. The grapes are direct pressed, the juice then settled to a low temperature and slow fermented in stainless steel or concrete vats. It's bottled at six to eight months. The fruit is fresh and vibrant, with a slight hint of salinity and a wonderful acidity.

Miraval rosé, from Provence, is one of the most popular, well-liked, and well-made rosé wines on the market. The grapes, a blend that includes Cinsault, Grenache, and Rolle, are direct pressed. Separately, Syrah is vinified partially by using the saignée method. The resulting wines are blended together and fermented in stainless steel vats (95 percent) and barrels (5 percent) with bâtonnage. The resulting wine is a salmon-colored pink, translucent, with notes of rose petals, fresh red fruit, a hint of salinity, and a lovely acidity to finish.

ROSATO FROM ITALY

Rosato is the Italian version of rosé. My favorites come from the Puglia region, but there are wonderful rosatos from all over Italy, including Etna in Sicily, and the Veneto in northeastern Italy, between the Dolomite Mountains and Adriatic Sea.

Kreos Negroamaro from Castello Monaci is made with 100 percent Negroamaro, an Italian grape, using the saignée method. A big, aromatic wine. Notes of tropical fruit and watermelon, bright strawberry and blood orange. A hint of fresh Bing cherry. Zesty acidity.

Also made with 100 percent Negroamaro is Contrade Rosato Salento IGT, redolent of strawberries and raspberries. Lovely hints of lemon and orange and an aftertaste of cranberry. Fruity yet dry, and incredibly thirst quenching. A great food wine, but also a great sipper.

ROSÉ MADE FROM MALBEC

Argentina and Chile both make great Malbec. They also make some lovely rosés from the same grape. The color is much more intense, and the jammyness you admire in a South American Malbec carries over to the rosés. Susana Balbo's Crios Rosé of Malbec from Argentina is an excellent example. Fresh strawberries and mixed berry jam come across the nose and the palate. A lovely spiciness helps finish out this lush rosé.

AMERICAN ROSÉS

In America, rosé is made from a number of different grapes. In the Northwest, Pinot Noir is the dominant rosé grape; on the East Coast, it's Cabernet Franc. And, of course, there are a bunch of others. That's what makes exploring wine so much fun.

West Coast

I discovered two of my favorite West Coast Pinot Noir rosés completely by accident. I arrived at Sokol Blosser Winery in Dayton, Oregon, without a reservation during the COVID pandemic. In August 2020, specially spaced tastings were permissible.

I got to the front door and the hostess asked if I had a reservation. I did not. I told her I would stand alone, or sit with another party, or wait. I knew it was bad, I explained, and was willing to take my punishment. She apologized, saying that they were fully booked, and that there was no way they could accommodate me, legally. California officials were roving the countryside, making sure wineries were not breaking the COVID serving rules. Having recently sold my own winery, I completely understood. I thanked her, and walked away a few feet, looking at my phone for the nearest winery.

Two women had been standing behind me. The hostess asked for their reservation, which they promptly answered. I overheard her ask, "How many in your party?" They responded in unison, "Three!" Then one of them turned toward me and said, "Come on, buster, you're coming with us!" I looked behind me to see if it wasn't a joke. "We've got room, if you want," one of them said. I was elated, and I jumped at the chance. The hostess was laughing.

Teresa Dean and Stacy Guettinger Sharp were both teachers from Tacoma, Washington, on a girls' weekend, tasting in Oregon wine country. They also had reservations at nearby Stoller Family Estate. I was their guest for the day! We had a great time, and ended up having dinner together, late into the evening, eating al fresco at a local Italian restaurant. I was thrilled. Wine makes such memories possible.

Sokol Blosser Winery

Sokol Blosser's Rosé of Pinot Noir is made from 100 percent Pinot Noir harvested using their Pellenc machine harvester, which destems the grapes as it picks them. The juice receives four to six hours of skin contact, and is cool fermented for approximately two weeks in stainless steel tanks. The wine has a gorgeous nose of fresh strawberry, kiwi, and other tropical fruits, as well as a very floral touch to it. It ends with a hint of citrus and cranberry.

Stoller Family Estate

Rosé has been a cornerstone of Stoller's portfolio for more than a decade. Stoller, founded by Bill Stoller, a native of Dayton, Oregon, in 1993, was the world's first LEED Gold winery. Today it is still run by the family. Stoller has been producing their Stoller Family Estate Pinot

Noir Rosé for more than a decade. Made from 100 percent Pinot Noir, it offers incredible aromas. Pink grapefruit and orange zest lead off the nose, then fresh-cut strawberries, young cherries, white peaches, spice, and lime. Fruity and buzzy, with a refreshing, zippy finish, it is a satisfying glass of wine and a super sipper.

Texas

The Texas Hill Country is a hugely evolving wine region, producing some exceptional wines. Rosé wines in the region are made from a number of different grapes, including Mourvèdre, Montepulciano, Counoise, Cinsault, and Grenache. To me, it seems, Grenache and the GSM trinity (Grenache, Mourvèdre, and Syrah) are at the heart of the rosé wine offerings from the region.

McPherson Cellars Les Espines Rosé is a dry rosé made from 100 percent estate-grown Grenache—50 percent Grenache Noir and 50 percent Grenache Blanc. The wine opens with strawberries, cranberries, and flower petals. Light, bright red fruits open up on the palate, joined by citrus notes of orange and lemon. Lovely acidity makes the light fruit linger. A gorgeous, well-balanced wine. They also offer Mourvèdre Rosé and Les Copains Rosé (Mourvèdre, Carignan, Cinsault, Counoise, and Syrah). All are exquisite wines.

East Coast

Many of the quality producers up and down the East Coast make their rosés from Cabernet Franc, finding their inspiration in the Cabernet Franc rosés of France's Loire Valley. These wineries, generally speaking, produce pale, salmon-pink wines that brim with fresh cherries, fresh-cut strawberries, a hint of citrus, and a creamy finish.

A good example of such a wine is Charles Joguet Chinon Rosé. Domaine Charles Joguet was founded in 1957, and today is currently owned by the Genet family. This was a groundbreaking winery that began making single vineyard wines to spotlight local terroir long before others did. They also began to go organic in 2008, and achieved certification in 2018. They are one of the best producers of Cabernet Franc in the region. Charles Joguet Chinon Rosé exhibits all the classic traits of a Cabernet Franc rosé—raspberry, cherry, and strawberry all come through, with hints of herbs and great acidity. Well-balanced tannins and long, lingering flavor.

Wölffer Estate Vineyard

The largest producer of quality rosé on the East Coast is Wölffer Estate Vineyard. The winery's 175 acres, which are sustainably farmed, are in Sagaponack, New York. It is estimated that Wölffer sells more than 150,000 cases of rosé a year (pulling from several different grape sources from around the world, including Argentina and France).

Founded in 1988 by international financier Christian Wölffer, the vineyard quickly gained a reputation for rosé. Wölffer Estate Gold Label Rosé is made by the pairing of winemaker Roman Roth with his longtime collaborator, vineyard manager Richie Pisacano.

"Rosés, some consumers feel (inaccurately), are too minor to warrant critical attention," wrote wine writer and friend Howard G. Goldberg in *The New York Times*. "But rosés, too, have gravitas, and the bright hues of Wölffer's Francophile versions, copper-and-coral colored, caress the eye; as for refreshment, the rosé is to South Fork partygoers what fountains are to Italian gardens."

The Gold Label series highlights the fruit of the estate. Roth and Pisacano have long touted the maritime influences of the Southampton-based winery, which faces the Atlantic Ocean and the tip of Long Island Sound. Wölffer's Estate Rosé is a blend of grapes: 69 percent Merlot, 18 percent Cabernet Franc, 6 percent Chardonnay, 3 percent Cabernet Sauvignon, 2 percent Pinot Noir, and 1 percent each Pinot Gris and Riesling. It's got that classic salmon-pink color. Impressive floral notes mingle with tropical fruits and citrus, exploding with flavor and fragrance.

McCall Wines

McCall Whole Cluster Pinot Noir Rosé, from New York's North Fork of Long Island, is a stunning wine from one of the region's premiere producers. McCall specializes in Pinot Noir. This whole-cluster wine is a revelation. Floral at the outset. Fresh, intense raspberry and green apple. A hint of blood orange makes this a wine hard to beat! Soft, approachable, fruity.

Anthony Road Wine Company

One of the truly special rosés on the East Coast is the Anthony Road Rosé of Lemberger, made by the übertalented Peter Becraft. This Finger Lakes rosé is a mouthful of fruit. It exhibits lovely notes of strawberry and cherry, but as Lenn Thompson wrote, "With layers of grapefruit, peach, kumquat, raspberries, candied ginger, lime, and even a little tamarind, it's incredibly complex with bright, citrusy acidity and a long, dry finish that shows just a little spice."

Fox Run Vineyards

From one of the most celebrated vineyards of the Finger Lakes, Fox Run Dry Rosé is a blend of 38 percent Lemberger, 35 percent Pinot Noir, and 27 percent Cabernet Franc. "Aromas of strawberry, melon, and white flowers with beautiful, well-integrated acidity and a bit more mid-palate concentration than many wines," wrote Lenn. I quite agree!

William Heritage Winery

William Heritage Winery makes the Reserve Rosé from grapes grown in the Outer Coastal Plain of New Jersey, the largest and most renowned AVA in the state and one of the oldest growing regions on the East Coast. It uses a blend of at least 50 percent Cabernet Franc and 25 percent Merlot, with another 15 percent Cabernet Sauvignon and 5 percent Syrah, though percentages change with each vintage. Strawberries, peaches, and lime wind their way through, with a hint of salinity.

Linganore Winecellars

Linganore Winecellars is one of the older Maryland wineries. Linganore Seventh is 100 percent Chambourcin, and named for Maryland being the seventh state admitted to the Union. Fresh-cut strawberry, bright raspberry, and green apples are up front. "Hints of limeade and just a bit of salinity on the finish," said Lenn.

Early Mountain Vineyards

Early Mountain Vineyards Rosé, made in Madison, Virginia, is a blend of early-picked Merlot, Petit Verdot providing color and depth, Malbec for bright acidity and fresher stone fruit aromas, Cabernet Franc for herbal and savory notes, and a "skosh of Syrah," according to the winemaker's notes. Strawberry and grapefruit come alive. Zippy acidity. Super refreshing.

Stinson Vineyards

Stinson's Rosé of Tannat, also from Virginia, is an absolute eye-opener. I love those big, deep, chewy reds that Tannat produces. But this was a surprising choice for a rosé wine. Bright young red fruit, accompanied by intense white peaches and a hint of grapefruit. Wonderful acidity and fruit on the finish. A robust food wine that can stand up to spice. A massive surprise and a must try!

SPARKLING WINES

The most memorable meal I ever had was at Domaine Chandon in Napa Valley. Three years after opening the winery, in 1977, the sparkling house debuted their high-end, white tablecloth food destination, The Restaurant at Domaine Chandon. The name was later changed to Étoile. Udo Nechutnys was the original chef, followed by Philippe Jeanty, Chris Manning, and Perry Hoffmann, the last two running it from 2007 until its closing in 2014 and garnering a Michelin star.

We arrived with a reservation for lunch. Back then, in the late 1990s, it was as special as a place could be. We ordered a flight of vintage sparkling wines, as well as glasses of Blanc de Blanc, Blanc de Noir, and sparkling rosé. Our waiter suggested foods from the menu based on our wine selections. We ordered shellfish and a salmon tray to start. I had a steak and Dominique the roast chicken.

For me, it was the day sparkling wine really came to life. With each sip, I appreciated the differences between the vintages, and between the styles. I was absolutely floored. The lunch was like a long lesson in sparkling wine, in the most enjoyable of ways. It was, simply put, eye-opening. And the food pairings were off the charts!

One of my favorite sparkling wines today is Domaine Chandon's Étoile Brut, from Chardonnay, Pinot Noir, and Pinot Meunier, aged and incredibly well-made. Fresh-cut apple, Asian pear, and lemon curd are present, with a little ginger finish.

SPARKLING WINE 101

Most classic sparkling wine in North America is based on the French model from the famed Champagne region. The wines are made from Chardonnay and Pinot Noir, sometimes including Pinot Meunier (depending on the house). We're talking about dry sparkling wine, not Pétillant Naturel or Piquette or some other co-fermented wine.

There are several different classic styles presently being made in the United States:

Cuvée (in France known as cuvée de prestige) is the highest end of a sparkling wine house's list. There is no hard-and-fast rule as to what the process is for cuvée, but traditionally it is the first-run juices of Chardonnay and Pinot Noir, which are thought to be the best, purest expression of the fruit, blended together. However, it also might be a blend of the best wines to make the best possible high-end wine. This choice is left to the owner and winemaker. Cuvée is usually made from barrel-aged wines, which offer bigger mouthfeel, immense richness, layered flavors, and enhanced ageability. One of the best producers on the East Coast, Lenz Winery of Long Island, for example, offers their cuvée six years after harvest; thus, their 2016 Cuvée was offered in late 2022.

Blanc de Noir (meaning "white from black," in essence white wine from black grapes) is a white wine made entirely of Pinot Noir, Pinot Meunier, or a blending of the two. Remember, the interiors of red or other dark grapes are the same color as white grapes. The color of the wine comes from contact with the skins. Thus, the Pinot Noir (or Pinot Meunier) is pressed whole cluster, and the juice that comes out of the press is basically a white wine, since the juice is not allowed to sit on the skins. This traditionally produces a medium- to dark-golden wine of immense flavor and complexity.

Blanc de Blanc (meaning "white from white," a white wine made from white grapes) is a sparkling wine made from Chardonnay.

Rosé is usually made by allowing some of the fresh-run Pinot Noir to sit on the skins for a while, then adding it to the sparkling wine blend for a blush of color. Only Chardonnay and Pinot Noir (and sometimes Pinot Meunier) are used.

Degrees of Dryness in Sparkling Wines

There are different levels assigned to describe the sweetness of a sparkling wine. The most common are:

Brut (less than 12 grams of sugar per liter)

Extra dry (between 12 and 17 grams)

Sec (between 17 and 32 grams)

Demi-sec (between 32 and 50 grams)

Doux (50 grams)

PUTTING THE SPARKLE IN SPARKLING WINE

In the méthode champenoise (or méthode traditionnelle), the wine is fermented and aged in a barrel. Lots are chosen, and the wine is assembled and placed in bottles. Before capping the bottles, fresh yeast and sugar are inserted. This causes a second fermentation in the bottle, which results in carbonation. After a period of time (six months to a year and a half, as a general rule), the bottles are placed upside down, so the yeast and any remaining particles settle against the cap. By this time, the secondary fermentation has created the bubbles we are familiar with. The bottles are then inserted into an ice bath (or a bed of dry ice) until the necks are frozen. Each cap is popped, and a little ice block shoots out, clearing the wine of any floating items. This process is known as disgorgement. The bottles are then leveled up with older wine and a small dose of sugar, and properly corked. The wine will wait again for some time before being released.

In the charmat method, the wine is put in a pressurized tank (called a bright tank) and injected with CO_2 to create the bubbles.

AMERICAN SPARKLERS

Here are some of my favorite sparkling wines by region.

California

Mumm Napa Brut Prestige is the house's signature sparkling wine. An exceptional California version of the French winery's classic wine.

J Vineyards & Winery's J Cuvée 20 from the Russian River Valley of Sonoma Valley is wonderful, with notes of stone fruit and lemon meringue, and a creamy finish.

Iron Horse Wedding Cuvée is a kind of Blanc de Noir, Pinot Noir blended with a touch of stainless-steel Chardonnay. Harvested by hand and whole-cluster pressed. Fantastic.

Roederer Estate, in Mendocino County, Anderson Valley, was founded by the great French house in 1982. Its all-estate brut is in the classic Champagne style.

J. Schram Blancs comes from Schramsberg, a winery that was originally founded in 1862 but fell into disrepair, and was revived in 1965. This is an incredible expression of Blanc de Blanc and one of their highest-end offerings.

Scribe Estate Sparkling Mission is an exciting new wine made using the Mission grape, an old vinifera historically associated with the Spanish missions in the New World.

Domaine Carneros Brut Rosé (an offshoot of the French house Taittinger) is a classic Chardonnay and Pinot Noir blend. Crisp, fruity, elegant. Domaine Carneros Le Rêve Rosé, 55 percent estate-grown Pinot Noir and 45 percent estate-grown Chardonnay, is out of this world but hard to come by. A soft coral—hued wine, it sparkles with fresh strawberry, apricot, grapefruit, and notes of ginger.

W. Donaldson Sonoma Blanc de Blancs and Rob McNeill Russian River Valley Brut Rosé are other California favorites.

Washington and Oregon

Sokol Blosser Blossom Ridge Sparkling Rosé of Pinot Noir Eola–Amity Hills is my top favorite out of Dayton, Oregon, in the Red Hills of Dundee in Yamhill County. Made from estate-grown Pinot Noir, this fantastic sparkler pours with a lovely pink mousse up at the top. Fresh and lively with strawberry and lime, it is a gorgeous, lip-smacking, tiny-bubbled beauty.

Argyle Extended Tirage Brut is their top-flight sparkler, aged for a decade on the yeast. Argyle's sparkling library of wines still aging on the yeast dates all the way back to their first vintage in 1987. One of the premiere sparkling winemakers in Oregon.

Soter Mineral Springs Brut Rosé from Soter Vineyards in Carlton, Oregon, is made from biodynamically estate-grown fruit, 81 percent Pinot Noir and 19 percent Chardonnay, and rests on the yeast for at least three years. Great fruit up front, lots of layers, and a nice hint of creaminess.

RMS Brut from ROCO Winery, Oregon's other sparkling-wine house, is named after Rollin M. Soles, who founded Argyle before moving to ROCO. The wine is made from Chardonnay and Pinot Noir grown in the Willamette Valley. Bright, fresh Granny Smith and Red Delicious apples, along with notes of lemon and lime, and a hint of grapefruit.

Some notable wines from Washington include Treveri Cellars Sparkling Rosé from Columbia Valley, and XOBC Cellars XO Bubby Rosé from Seattle.

New Mexico, Colorado & Texas

Gruet Brut NV is made in New Mexico, an extension of Gilbert Gruet's Champagne house in Bethon, France. They've been making wine here for more than 25 years and are one of the biggest and best producers of sparkling wine in the United States. Granny Smith apple, lemon curd, and key lime pie all blend in one lovely, bone-dry sparkler.

Carboy Grand Blanc de Blanc is the best of Washington and Colorado (where the wine is made), starting with its blend of grapes: 28 percent Orange Muscat, 27 percent Riesling, 15 percent Albariño, 12 percent Roussanne, 11 percent Viognier, 5 percent Sauvignon Blanc, and 2 percent Pinot Gris. Fruit forward and so much fun to drink! I also love their Native Fizz Sparkling Rosé (33 percent each Verona, Aromella, and Vignoles), which resonates with tropical fruit, fresh-cut apple, cranberry, cantaloupe, and clementine.

McPherson Sparkling Wine from Lubbock, Texas, starts with a lovely, foamy mousse that lasts, with notes of baked pastry and lemon zest. One hundred percent Chenin Blanc makes this a standout!

What Is Mousse?

Mousse in French means foam or froth. It often refers to foods that are whipped, like egg whites. When a Champagne or sparkling wine is poured, a small head made up of tiny bubbles forms at the top of the flute, much like a head on beer. This is referred to as a mousse. Sometimes it dissipates quickly, but a fine mousse may linger longer.

New York

New York State has long had a good reputation for sparkling wine. In fact, for many years, the preferred American sparkling was Gold Seal Winery, made in the Finger Lakes. The winery was headed by the famous Charles Fournier, who left Veuve Clicquot Ponsardin to establish one of the great sparkling wine programs in North America. Fournier worked closely with such East Coast wine titans as Philip Wagner and Dr. Konstantin Frank. Today, New York continues to make some stunning sparklers in each of its big three regions.

Finger Lakes

Dr. Konstantin Frank Brut is made from 55 percent Chardonnay, 40 percent Pinot Noir, and 5 percent Pinot Meunier, all grown on Keuka Lake. The grapes are harvested by hand and gently pressed; 2 percent of the Pinot Noir is barrel fermented in French oak. Dr. Konstantin Frank Winery was founded in 1962, its extensive sparkling program begun by Willy Frank in the late 1980s. The high-quality wines made there by Eric Bauman over the past decade and a half have transformed the winery into a top-tier producer.

Keuka Spring Vineyards produces the finely crafted Zweigelt Traditional Method Sparkling, made by Dan Bissell.

Red Tail Ridge Sparkling Rosé is made by Mike Schnelle and Nancy Irelan on the shores of Seneca Lake. Formerly of E. & J. Gallo Winery, Irelan is turning out a solid line of still wines and a growing list of sparklers. This rosé includes notes of bright sour cherry and fresh-cut strawberries, with hints of blood orange. It has a lovely pink mousse.

Lamoreaux Landing Blanc de Blanc is made from estate vineyard blocks of Chardonnay and Pinot Noir grown on the east side of Seneca Lake. It shows delicate pear and lemon flavors with layers of toasted bread complexity. It has a lively acid structure and a lingering creamy finish. Refreshing and refined. Glenora Wine Cellars, also on Seneca Lake, makes very solid sparklers, including Glenora Riesling Sparkling Wine.

Heart & Hands Brut Rosé hails from Union Spring. Owned by Susan and Tom Higgins, the winery is one of the best producers of still wines, but their sparkler is a revelation, made from 100 percent Pinot Noir. Aromatic, bright, fruity, sophisticated, and bone-dry. Swedish Hill Blanc de Blanc is made by the Peterson family, also on Cayuga Lake. Surprisingly wonderful green apple and a lemony finish. Terrific.

Hudson Valley

Tousey Winery The Loic Blanc de Blancs is an especially good wine. Made from 100 percent whole-cluster Chardonnay grapes, it is pressed at 34°F to preserve the freshness of the fruit. This sparkling wine is made using the méthode champenoise, and takes three years to mature in the bottle. Peach, green apple, and fresh apple compete with tropical notes, with hints of bread and spice swirled in. The wine ends with great acidity and a bit of creaminess. An excellent sparkler.

Brotherhood Winery, America's oldest, makes lovely sparkling wines; it's not surprising, as they've been doing it since 1839. Grand Monarque Cuvée is a traditional method sparkler, aged for a minimum of two years before disgorging, producing a brut with rich flavors and aromas. Their B Sparkling Chardonnay is fermented from 100 percent New York State Chardonnay grapes. Crisp acidity and bright fruit highlight this wine. A big nose full of pears with a light yeasty note. Nice minerality and a beautiful, long-lasting dry finish.

Whitecliff Vineyard & Winery's North River Blanc de Blanc is another excellent sparkling wine made in the classic style, as well as Galway Rock's Saratoga Sparkling Wine Co. Rosé Extra Dry.

Long Island

Lenz Méthode Traditionelle Cuvée comes from a winery founded in 1978; it has some of the most mature vineyards in the region. Their cuvée is a méthode champenoise sparkler made from 100 percent Pinot Noir. It has a big nose of yeast and apple and a whiff of something tropical. The 2005 offered bright white cherry with hints of apple and a touch of lime and kiwi. This wine has big flavor, great acidity, and a tremendous refreshing finish. One of the best and most elegant and complex sparkling wines made on the East Coast.

Sparkling Pointe is one of the best sparkling wine houses on the East Coast, and their winemaker, Gilles Martin, is a star. The brut and Blanc de Blancs are exceptional. And their big traditional method Brut Seduction can compete in any region.

Bedell Cellars Sparkling Rosé is an exceptional offering from Richard Olsen-Harbich, one of the East Coast's star winemakers. Paumanok Blanc de Blancs is also wonderful. Sannino Vineyard Vivacious Sparkling Wine is a 100 percent Cabernet Sauvignon rosé sparkler.

New England

Jones Family Farms' Whimsical White is a dry, aromatic, sparkling wine, a blend of 50 percent Vidal Blanc and 50 percent as-yet-unnamed hybrid of Riesling and Cayuga white grapes developed by Cornell University (and grown entirely in the Jones Family vineyards). The wine is cold fermented in stainless steel for seven to nine months, then carbonated and bottled using the charmat method. Right from the first whiff, this wine is a winner! White peach, tropical fruits, and honey are all strong on the nose and across the palate. Light and delicate. It has just a hint of pink citrus pop at the end, which gives it integrity. This is an absolutely wonderful sparkling wine, hailing from Connecticut.

In Massachusetts, Westport Rivers Brut Cuvée RJR is a classic New England sparkler. And there's also Black Birch Vineyard Brilliant Brut, made from a blend of grapes.

Mid-Atlantic and Virginia

There are some special sparklers from New Jersey. William Heritage Blanc de Noirs is exceptional, made from 100 percent estate-grown Pinot Noir. Hawk Haven Vineyard Méthode Champenoise Estate by Todd Wuerker is super impressive. His Fizz Nouveau Pinot Noir Rosé is fresh, bright, and refreshing.

Maryland offerings include Big Cork Vineyards Chenin Blanc Brut, a fantastic twist on classic sparkling wine, lively and lovely! Crow Vineyard on the Eastern Shore offers the fantastic Sparkling Barbera Rosé and a quaffable Sparkling Vidal Blanc, perfect for brunch and celebrations. There's also Linganore Winecellars Luminé Brut—aromatic, fun, fresh, and spritzy.

Thibaut-Janisson Xtra Brut is a classic tête de cuvée, meaning only the first-run juice. Made in Virginia from reserve barrel-aged wines, it is super dry and aromatic, with layers of flavors and complexity. Thibaut-Janisson Winery is one of the major sparkling houses of the East Coast. They also make a fantastic Blanc de Noirs and Blanc de Chardonnay, as well as the refreshing Virginia Fizz, a stainless steel Chardonnay, with bright apples, tropical fruit, and citrus. Dave McIntyre wrote in *The Washington Post*, "The T-J (a nice abbreviation given the implied reference to Thomas Jefferson and his love of wines) has become a darling of the Washington restaurant scene, because it is both local and top quality."

Veritas Scintilla Sparkling Wine and Veritas Sparkling Rosé are made in limited quantities and are special wines indeed. The winery, located in Afton, Virginia, is a family business owned by Andrew and Patricia Hodson, who make Scintilla from 100 percent Chardonnay. It is a rich, golden-colored wine with tiny, elegant bubbles. Lemon, green apple, and pear, accented by a touch of yeast and toasted brioche, all come through. Bright acidic finish and a nice lingering aftertaste.

Michigan and Ohio

That MAWBY is one of the premiere sparkling-wine houses in the country is slightly surprising because of its location in Suttons Bay, Michigan. Once you taste their wines, you forget about that. All you can think is, "How can I get more of that?" Mawby Sparkling 50th Anniversary Brut Cuvée is a méthode champenoise made with 100 percent Leelanau Peninsula Chardonnay and Riesling, and a touch of twenty-year-old French oak–aged spirits. Bright aromas and fresh flavors, but traditional complexity and elegance. Mawby Blanc Brut Méthode Champenoise, made from Leelanau Peninsula Chardonnay, Pinot Gris, and Riesling, is also amazing. The winery produces more than two dozen sparklers, from fun fizz to elegant, sophisticated wines. Mawby Sparkling Sex Brut Rosé is their flagship wine, made from a blend of grapes, and is well worth seeking out.

St. Julian Winery boasts a portfolio of almost a dozen sparklers. Their Braganini Reserve Blanc de Blanc is the big prize at the top of their line, and well worth the very affordable price. One hundred percent Michigan fruit. A sophisticated bubbly. St. Julian Ciao Bolle! Brut Rosé, pressed from Cabernet Sauvignon and Marquette, is a mix of fresh strawberries, tropical fruits, and lemonade, with grapefruit on the finish.

PÉTILLANT NATUREL AND PIQUETTE

Ever get the feeling things are going on around you, and you're the last to know? Pétillant Naturel. What is it? Where did it come from? Because, suddenly, it's everywhere! And if you're not drinking it, seemingly, you're not hip.

The truth is that Pétillant Naturel is one of the oldest frizzante styles of wine there is. It fell out of favor and now has suddenly been reborn. In English, it means "naturally bubbling." Pét Nats, as they have become known these days, are spritzy, fizzy, tingly wines in white, rosé, or red. They usually have about half the bubbles of traditional Champagne, and they are some of the easiest wines to make—that is, for sparkling wine.

Pét Nats are fantastic for lunch and brunch, a wonderful afternoon sipper. They are not meant to be fine wine, but rather a wine to be enjoyed.

PÉT NAT 101

When a winery crushes their grapes, the resulting juice has a lot of sugar in it, anywhere from 21 to 28 Brix (the Brix scale is used to measure sugar content). Yeasts are then added to the juice to begin the fermentation process. Yeasts feed on the sugar and convert it to carbon dioxide and alcohol. As they consume the sugar in the juice, the Brix level starts to go down and the alcohol content begins to rise.

Depending on the winemaker and the grapes, when the sugar level in the juice decreases to 6 to 2 Brix, that's when they'll get their plan in motion. Usually for a white or rosé sparkler, the wine is racked off and bottled. With red grapes, winemakers will usually start at 8 to 6 Brix; they'll press the must, let the wine settle briefly, and then bottle. All this takes anywhere from ten days to three weeks. At this point, there is still a minimal amount of sugar in the liquid.

The wine is capped, usually with a crown cap, like on a beer bottle. And then the fun begins, because the yeast don't rest. They keep eating. And making alcohol. And making bubbles. And by the time all the sugar in the liquid is gone, you have an 11 to 12 percent alcohol wine with a nice amount of fizz.

The natural wine community embraced the idea of re-introducing Pét Nat because little to no SO_2 is added, as the sulfites might retard the effectiveness of the yeast. It's a win-win for natural winemakers. And it gives Pét Nat a wonderful, new artisanal feel.

Here's where style comes in. Some winemakers will leave the wine cloudy, with sediment in the bottle, and call it a day. In France, this is also known as the méthode ancestrale (a term you might see on a label). This is classic Pét Nat.

Others will disgorge the bottles; this process involves placing the bottles upside down in ice water or in dry ice. The dead yeast cells collect there and freeze; the winemaker then pops the cap and the detritus and dead yeast are displaced. The bottle is topped off with a sweet wine or a dry wine (much like Champagne or traditional sparkling winemakers do). In this way, they remove some but not all of the sediment. The bottles are recapped and left to re-ferment any extant sugars. Another difference between Champagne and Pét Nats is that Champagne usually ages in cellars for years before and after disgorgement. Pét Nats are bottled and put up for sale about six months later, tops.

Most Pét Nats have some degree of sediment in them. These are rustic wines. But they are wonderful. Uncomplicated. Fun.

Served chilled like their more refined brethren, Pét Nats sparkle both literally and figuratively. Yes, they are bubbly. And while the wines are dry, they tend to exhibit lovely fruit flavors. And more and more, winemakers feel free to try all kinds of grapes. While traditional Champagne is bound by Chardonnay and Pinot Noir, there are no rules with Pét Nats. These lovely sparklers are made from Albariño, Sauvignon Blanc, Riesling, Malbec, Marquette, and all manner of grapes for new and fun wines.

Old Westminster Winery

Old Westminster Winery in Maryland is generally acknowledged to be the very best producer of Pétillant Naturel on the East Coast, and probably in America. I first became aware of Old Westminster Winery in 2013. The Baker siblings, Drew, Lisa, and Ashli, manage the vineyard, make the wine, and market it. There are two things you need to know about Lisa Hinton (her married name). She is incredibly charming, funny, witty, and sarcastic, and very gracious. And she knows how to make wine. When she speaks, people listen. So imagine my thrill when I got to sit next to Lisa and across the table from Dave McIntyre of *The Washington Post* at a mid-Atlantic wine tasting in Pennsylvania in 2017.

The first Pét Nat of hers I tasted was their Pétillant Naturel Syrah Rosé 2015. The nose of this spontaneous fermentation Pét Nat was a combination of apples and fresh bread, with a lovely effervescence and tremendous acidity, a very light rosé made from estate vineyard Syrah. According to Lisa, the wine was disgorged and the lees and dead yeast cells displaced with new wine, "but we sacrificed a lot of wine in the process." They made seventy cases of this wonderful wine, with hints of bright strawberry and raspberry and lots of citrus zest, with a creamier finish than I expected. Since then, I've tried a number of her other Pét Nats, including a Grüner Veltliner, Barbera Rosé, and Gamay Rosé.

Take home a bottle, pop it in the fridge, and enjoy it with a friend or loved one or all of the above. Don't take it too seriously—it's just wine!

Greenvale Vineyards

Greenvale Vineyards produces its wines on the family's farm, which was established in 1863 and is located on Aquidneck Island in Rhode Island, overlooking Newport Bay, not far, nautically, from the North Shore of Long Island.

Billy Wilson, son of the owners, is a very talented winemaker. They grow Chardonnay, Cabernet Franc, and a number of other vinifera grapes. They also grow Albariño. Their excellent still wine Albariño, fermented and made in stainless steel, is fruit forward, with hints of white peach, spice, and citrus. They also make a limited release Albariño Pét Nat. The wine is disgorged, so the final bottle has a lovely liquid that is something special. It is bright with tropical fruit and aromatics, and exhibits fine, sparkling bubbles that are simply exquisite.

Red Tail Ridge Winery

Located in New York's Finger Lakes, this winery is owned by Nancy Irelan and her husband, Mike Schnelle. Nancy has been in the wine industry for more than 35 years, including working as a winemaker at E. & J. Gallo Winery and as a researcher in the Viticulture and Enology Department at UC Davis.

Red Tail Ridge Pétillant Naturel Sparkling Pinot Noir Rosé is one of the prettiest Pét Nats you will ever try, complete with a lovely, pink mousse. For those who like sparkling rosé wines, this one is exceptional, with the requisite aromas and flavors of bright strawberries, bright cherries, and key lime pie. It has lovely acidity and terrific flavor. I have celebrated many special occasions with this wine.

Birichino

Birichino was established by Alex Krause and John Locke in Santa Cruz in 2008. They produce a number of what they term "Pétulant Naturels," a humorous twist on the style's name. They make Chenin Blanc, Cinsault, Malvasia Bianca, skin-fermented Malvasia Bianca, Carignan, and Zinfandel varietal bottlings. Birichino 2020 Pétulant Naturel Malvasia Bianca is made from the fruit of vines that are more than thirty years old. This slightly cloudy wine drinks like grapefruit soda! There are hints of tropical fruits, nectarine, floral notes, and a zesty citrus finish. It's super thirst quenching, like an alcoholic grapefruit Orangina. An absolutely lovely wine, perfect to serve for brunch or throughout the day. Any of the Birichino Pét Nats are absolutely worth the price.

PIQUETTE

Piquette is another farm-style wine that has seen a resurgence over the last decade. It employs a winemaking process that dates back to the ancient Greeks and Romans, who used it to make wine for common folk and slaves. Later, in France and Italy, estate workers would make this style of wine. Piquette is the French term for the wine, while the Italians call it acqua pazza and vinello.

The grapes are pressed, then rehydrated with water and allowed to re-ferment. Some makers simply add water, which leads to a wine that is much lower in alcohol. Others add sugar or fruit juice (especially apple) to incorporate some flavor and alcohol during the re-fermentation process. Others also add raisins or other fruits for flavor. No extra yeast is usually added, since the wine has already fermented once, and the yeast usually stays active. The result is a lighter style of wine. There are very good Piquettes being made; some are still, but most are frizzante, or sparkling.

Wild Arc Farm

Todd Cavallo, co-owner of Wild Arc Farm in Pine Bush, New York, is credited with bringing this country-style wine back to popularity. His introduction of it to the US market was such a hit that he was named one of *Wine Enthusiast*'s 40 Under 40 Tastemakers in 2019. Cavallo and his wife, Crystal, began Wild Arc in 2016, a ten-acre biodynamic, permaculture-focused farm. They make impressive wines and ciders from locally sourced apples and grapes, as well as from their own grapes. Wild Arc Farm Piquette! Sparkling Rosato is a light pink bombshell of a wine, fizzy, zippy, and refreshing. It has notes of light strawberry and orange zest, and terrific tingly acid.

Bluemont Vineyard

Bluemont Vineyard, located in Bluemont, Virginia, is owned by the Zurschmeide family. They make some of the best Piquettes I have ever had. Their Bluemont Piquette Blanc is a revelation, made from the pomace of Albariño grapes. First, water is added and it is fermented to low alcohol, then some fully fermented Albariño wine is added for final flavor. It is an unfiltered wine, with a hint of sweetness and a lovely, delicate effervescence. The nose abounds with tropical fruit notes, as well as lychee and pear, and a bit of lemon custard.

Beneduce Vineyards

Mike Beneduce is the intrepid vineyardist and mad winemaker at this winery in Pittstown, New Jersey. He was named *Edible Jersey*'s Beverage Artisan of the Year and Outstanding Young Farmer of the Year by the New Jersey State Board of Agriculture. Mike's offering is his famous Beneduce Acqua Pazza. This low-alcohol, semitransparent pink wine is modeled on the Italian aperitivo. Beneduce uses pressed Blaufränkisch skins and raw wildflower honey from local honey provider Zach & Zoë Sweet Bee Farm. The resulting wine has notes of bright cherry and grapefruit, and a lovely citrus finish. Super refreshing.

Troon Vineyard

Troon Vineyard is owned by Denise and Dr. Bryan White, who came to the Applegate Valley in Oregon in early 2017. Craig Camp is general manager, with more than three decades of experience in the wine industry, and Nate Wall is winemaker.

Troon Vineyard Piquette! Méthode Ancestrale Applegate Valley is made after the pressing of their estate white and rosé wines. These estate grapes are then re-fermented in stainless steel. Troon uses native yeast for their fermentations. This new second wine is quickly bottled under crown caps to finish fermentation in the bottle. It is delicate, fresh, and fizzy with bright fruit flavors, hints of strawberry and orange, and a lovely light pink-salmon color. Perfect for brunch or lunch, or as an aperitif.

CO-FERMENTED WINES

Co-ferments are an ever-evolving category, with origins in agriculture, when farmers would make field blends, using small amounts of white grapes grown side by side with red varieties, to add softness and aroma to their red wines. Such wines remain one of the backbones of classic winemaking.

The boundaries of co-ferments, like the universe, keep expanding. More current iterations have blurred the lines between wine, cider, and beer in the New World. You may hear "co-ferment" bandied about by natural wine producers, or biodynamic craftsmen, or larger commercial producers. It belongs to no one group, and what a co-ferment is has changed so much in the last decade it'll make your head spin.

My experience with the category evolved. I first approached it as a wine lover and novice, then as a wine geek, and finally as a curious winemaker working alongside some very innovative people. Todd Cavallo (along with his wife, Crystal Cornish) of Wild Arc and Andy Brennan (and his wife, Polly Giragosian) of Aaron Burr Cidery, both of the Hudson Valley, were among the early influencers in the category.

Like anything else, I had to find my own way, as there are good and bad examples out there. But the category is only growing. And it's super fun!

OLD-SCHOOL CO-FERMENTS: CÔTE-RÔTIE

What is co-fermentation? Many wines are blends, which means that the grape types are fermented separately, then blended together at a later date. Co-fermentation is when two or more grape varieties are fermented together. Sometimes the grapes are pressed together, sometimes separately, then the juices are combined. Either way, the juices are fermented together in tanks (and then barrels).

"For centuries, grape varieties grew side by side in a vineyard," wrote Shelby Vittek for *Wine Enthusiast*. "At harvest, the interplanted grapes are picked and co-fermented together. The flavor profile of field blends varies depending on the grapes they contain, but they're prized for a level of balance, harmony and complexity."

"Co-fermentation, a more intentional practice, developed in regions like Rioja and Tuscany, where a small percentage of white grapes was used to soften the tannins of red varieties (e.g., Chianti Classico was historically a co-ferment of Sangiovese with the indigenous red grape Canaiolo Nero as well Trebbiano and Malvasia)," explained Nikki Goddard for the Napa Valley Wine Academy. Today, the region of Côte-Rôtie in France is considered ground zero for great examples of this type of winemaking.

In the early 2000s, I fell in love with Rhône and Rhône-styled wines—Châteauneuf-du-Pape, Hermitage and Croze Hermitage, Gigondas, and Côte-Rôtie. I had no in-depth knowledge of the region and relied very much on the recommendations of *Wine Spectator*, Robert Parker, and *Wine Enthusiast*. One of my favorite bottles was a J. Vidal-Fleury Côte-Rôtie La Chatillone, which is traditionally Syrah with up to 12 percent Viognier. Its addition gives the wine a strong floral note. The finished wine radiates violets and blueberries, as well as cassis and raspberry, foretelling a beautifully supple wine, soft and approachable. It was a major purchase. What I didn't understand until after I bought it, and my then wife and I consumed it, was that it was a co-ferment of Syrah and Viognier. This was a major stepping stone in our appreciation of this technique.

It is important to note that co-fermented Côte-Rôtie wines are a small part of the offerings of the Côte-Rôtie region, and an even smaller portion of the wines that come from the Rhône. But they provide an exceptional experience and flavor.

I similarly fell in love with E. Guigal Côte-Rôtie Brune et Blonde, which is typically Syrah with as much as 4 to 5 percent Viognier. And I also enjoyed the lighter-styled E. Guigal Côte-Rôtie La Mouline, which can be up to 12 percent Viognier. This is a classic old-world wine experience. FYI, Brune means the wine is 100 percent Syrah; Brune et Blonde means it contains Viognier. The region's winemaking laws allow for the inclusion of up to 20 percent Viognier.

These wines and their subsequent imitators around the world influenced our direction when J. Stephen Casscles and I started making wine together in the Hudson Valley.

NEW SPINS ON TRADITIONAL CO-FERMENTATION

In the late 1980s and early 1990s, a largely West Coast group of American winemakers attempted to simulate the wines of the Rhône region, using the same grapes and techniques, to make wines with an American twist. Syrah exploded in the United States. The most famous of these winemakers were Randall Grahm of Bonny Doon Vineyard and Bob Lindquist of Qupé Wine Cellars. I was a devout Grahm follower, as he made one insanely great, innovative wine after another. And he was an amazing promoter—his "funeral for the cork" publicity stunt in 2002, dropping corks for screw-cap closures, sent the wine world into a tizzy. Soon, many regions were making wonderful co-ferments similar to those from Côte-Rôtie.

Clendenen Family Vineyards

Clendenen Family Vineyards Rancho La Cuna Syrah-Viognier features about 10 percent Viognier. Their Rancho La Cuna Vineyard is located in one of my favorite winemaking regions in the world, between the Santa

Maria and Santa Ynez Valleys in California. This wine is aged in Hungarian oak for approximately five years before bottling. The wine is super aromatic, exploding with blackberries and violets, with notes of soft spice, finishing with black pepper and lingering dark fruit. Soft and aromatic, these delicate wines are absolutely beautiful.

Yering Station

Yering Station is a historic winery located in Victoria, in the Yarra Valley of Australia. The Scottish-born Ryrie brothers planted the first vines in 1838 on 43,000 acres. In 1850, the plantings were expanded. The Rathbone family now owns this iconic winery. Yering Station Shiraz-Viognier is a blend of 98 percent Shiraz and 2 percent Viognier. It has lush notes of stewed dark fruits and great tannins. Soft and delicious, super smooth, elegant, and well-balanced.

Ridge Vineyards

Ridge Vineyards is another of the great wine estates in California. They have two sites, the original at Monte Bello Ridge in Santa Clara County in the Santa Cruz Mountains AVA, and the Lytton Springs vineyards in the Dry Creek Valley AVA of Sonoma County. Ridge Vineyards' 1971 Monte Bello Cabernet Sauvignon was well received at the historic 1976 "Judgment of Paris" wine tasting. Wine has been made at the Monte Bello site since 1892, but Ridge Vineyards was founded in 1960 by a group of Stanford Research Institute engineers. Ridge Vineyards Lytton Estate Syrah from the Dry Creek Valley is 100 percent organic and generally a blend of 93 percent Syrah and 7 percent Viognier. A stunning wine that is highly rated every year.

Okanagan Crush Pad Narrative

Okanagan Crush Pad Narrative Syrah Viognier is made in the Okanagan Valley in British Columbia. Their Narrative line of wines is low intervention and meant to reflect the terroir of the region. I love this wine, which is 85 percent Syrah and 15 percent Viognier and aged in the newly popular concrete eggs. They leave this wine on the skins for approximately nine months, which gives it real complexity and softness. Notes of violets and plums, raspberry and strawberry. The fruit lingers. Beautiful and round.

FUNKY NEW CO-FERMENTS

Today, small artisanal producers have stretched the boundaries and revived ancient traditions of co-ferments and field blends. They are no longer limited to Syrah and Viognier.

Montezuma Winery

Phil Plummer is one of the most exciting and versatile young winemakers on the scene in the Finger Lakes in New York. He makes a small lake of quaffable table wine that is affordably priced and super popular. But juxtaposed to this is his Voleur line. By relying on time-honored techniques and adding his own spin, Phil set out to build novel wines with old souls. He'll try any technique or combination that strikes his fancy (voleur means "thief" in French). And more often than not, he pulls it off! His Lemberger Co-Ferment (with Grüner Veltliner) is a red stunner, with bright, jammy fruit, real depth, a nice earthiness, and a wonderful finish. It's made in limited quantities and sells out fast. But these kinds of wines are popping up all over America.

Barry Family Cellars

Ian Barry is the coolest garagiste, with a trucker hat, sunglasses, a beard, and a turntable. This young Finger Lakes winemaker is producing some of the wildest, most out there wines on the East Coast. A garagiste is a winemaker who is doing things in small batches, out of the mainstream. It started out as a movement in Bordeaux in the late 1980s and early 1990s, as a reaction to big commercial wines being overmanipulated. Ian, a friend of mine, works as the winemaker at Six Eighty Cellars on Cayuga Lake. But he also puts out his own line of wines under the Barry Family Cellars label. His Four Track Demo is a co-ferment of four grape varieties, which change each year. The release with Blaufränkisch, Cabernet Franc, Chardonnay, and Cabernet Sauvignon was simply amazing. No matter the combo, this wine is soft but flavorful with long-lasting fruit. A wonderful sipper and perfectly paired with lighter fare.

L'Erta di Radda

Diego Finocchi, owner/winemaker of L'Erta di Radda in Chianti, Italy, makes Due & Due IGT Rosso Toscana with classic Italian grapes—70 percent Sangiovese (red) and Canaiolo (red), and 30 percent Trebbiano (white) and Malvasia (white). The grapes come from a vineyard planted in 1971 and are fermented in whole clusters in stainless steel. The wine is later aged 50 percent in stainless steel and 50 percent in cement tanks. "Blending red and white grapes together to make a unique wine is something that has always fascinated me," said Finocchi. "I use white grapes to slim the wine down, soften the Sangiovese's tannins, while at the same time creating a more complex aromatic profile." The final wine has tons of fresh fruit, is lush with red bright berries and floral notes, and is supple and easy to drink.

BRAVE NEW WORLD: THE CUTTING EDGE

The term "co-ferment" has happily been co-opted to extend to other combinations—grapes and cider, grapes and beer, grapes and mead—greatly widening its meaning. In the Northeast, the lines have been especially blurred with the plethora of wineries, breweries, distilleries, cideries, meaderies, and fermentories that have popped up. The region has spawned important initiatives worldwide, including collaborations and co-fermentations that stretch the meanings of established beverage categories. Many other regions are taking part as well.

"Fruit wines are an embodiment of a recent blurring of borders across fermentation categories, a radical break from tradition," wrote Jess Lander in the *San Francisco Chronicle*. "Many winemakers are doing these experiments simply because it's fun and creative. Others see it as a sustainable initiative for the future, as a stopgap for production in drought or fire-ridden years."

"There's a whole cultural shift where beer is becoming wine-like, kombucha is becoming beer-like and wine is becoming beer-like," said Napa winemaker Steve Matthiasson of Matthiasson Wines.

"By blending the two seemingly opposite worlds of beer and wine together, we've discovered that they collide quite nicely," noted Sam Calagione, founder of Dogfish Head Brewery.

"The revival of legacy processes and their convergence with innovative approaches to cold-climate grape varieties, ciders, fruit wines and co-fermentation is really just beginning, so heads up and be ready to taste what's coming," says Todd Trzaskos, a highly respected New England craft industry journalist.

Aaron Burr Cidery

Among the first of these that I recall was Aaron Burr Cidery's Appinette. In 2014, there was no question that, among foodies, this was the absolute darling of the farm-to-table world. A "unicorn cider," as wine writer Lenn Thompson referred to it, it was being served at such tony restaurants as Eleven Madison Park and Gramercy Tavern, was on the wine list at the Culinary Institute of America at Hyde Park, and sold at upscale food emporiums like Eataly and Murray's Cheese in New York City.

The cidery, located in Wurtsboro, New York, was founded by Andy Brennan and his wife, Polly. Aaron Burr Appinette was the first co-ferment that crossed the line—mixing grape and fruit juice. It is made from 30 percent Finger Lake Traminette grapes and 70 percent Orange County (New York) apples (70 percent of those are Idared, Russet, and Spy—the rest of the apples are foraged). It's a dry cider with a floral aroma that one assumes comes from the Traminette. It's a light amber color, like a nice aged Champagne, with medium carbonation and a suggestion of cloudiness and a hint of grapefruit at the end. It is fantastic. And it set the local wine scene on edge.

Folklor Wine & Cider

A few miles from Lake Michigan, at their 52-acre home farm in Charlevoix, Michigan, the husband-and-wife team of Derrick Vogel and Izabela Babinska tend cold-hardy and hybrid grapes, as well as their heirloom apple and pear orchards.

Derrick was a laboratory scientist, and Iza was a grant developer. The two visited New Zealand, went to a winery, and fell in love. They returned to Michigan and started working the tasting rooms of the Petoskey Wine Region. Today, Izabela, born in Poland, is the grape grower and business manager of Folklor, armed with her MBA. Having grown up on a dairy farm, Derrick helps grow the grapes and is the winemaker.

Ode to Home was made from their L'Acadie Blanc grapes blended with Sommerset of Maine apples, and wild yeast fermented. The resulting wine is a Pét Nat–styled co-ferment that is unfined and unfiltered, with no sulfites added. It is slightly funky but also juicy and delicious!

North American Press

North American Press is located in Santa Rosa, California. Their Wildcard Wild Grape Dry Sparkling Cider is the brainchild of owner/winemaker Matt Niess. Wildcard is a wild ride. It is a co-ferment of heirloom organic-certified Gravenstein apples and Russian River foraged wild grapes. Niess was inspired by La Garagista in Vermont. This is farmhouse cider/wine making. Hints of apple pie, fresh peach, and mixed nuts come through. Also notes of salted watermelon. It's slightly sparkling, bone-dry, and soft, complex, and elegant. Very refreshing.

Domaine du Nival

Saison du Coteau Gamaret is a barrel-aged wheat saison macerated on Gamaret grape pomace, made by Domaine du Nival in Saint-Louis, Quebec, just northeast of Montreal, which produces wines, ciders, and beers. They prefer natural fermentations, and bottle their products unfined and unfiltered, with minimal use of sulfur. This beer/wine is produced in microbatches. The color is a light pink, and it is slightly effervescent. Fruity, with notes of melon and a hint of bready yeast. A great patio sipper, especially during the summer.

Dogfish Head Brewery

Sam Calagione, founder of Dogfish Head Brewery with his wife, Mariah, has been making co-fermented beers for a long time. A maverick from the very beginning of his brewing career, Sam is outspoken and admired. "We've been experimenting with grape juice and must in the brewing process with beers like Midas Touch, Red & White, Noble Rot, and Sixty One since we first opened twenty-three years ago as the smallest American craft brewery," said Calagione.

Dogfish Head Mixed Media is a saisonesque co-ferment of 51 percent grain and 49 percent Viognier grapes from Alexandria Nicole Cellars in Prosser, Washington. The 51 percent grain ensures it will be called beer rather than wine. This aromatic co-ferment uses a distinctive Belgian yeast strain. With big notes of melon and bright white grapes, it's crisp, dry, and tart. A terrific alternative for fans of aromatic white wines.

FRUIT WINES

I am constantly amazed at how people roll their eyes at this category. Paul Vigna, the highly thought of mid-Atlantic wine writer, holds an annual confab for winemakers and wine influencers. He called me before one meeting and asked if there were any wineries I could recommend. I suggested a fruit winemaker, Hermit Woods. He chuckled. Knowing the seriousness of the attending wine crowd, he thought it would be something fun and different. During the presentation, people raised their eyebrows and looked questioningly at each other. What were these guys doing at such a high-end winemakers' meet? Then they tasted the dry white and the dry red, and the eyeballs started rolling again. Many insisted there must be grapes in these wines, that they were too complex, too flavorful, too well constructed. Disbelief reigned.

However, years before, my former brother-in-law, Michael Hoover, and his wife, Jill, lived in Maine with their three golden retrievers. Over the years, we had gone up to visit them a number of times—and, of course, I always had to satisfy my fix for Maine wines, some of which are very good.

The most notable Maine winery to me is also Maine's first, Bartlett Maine Estate Winery, founded by Robert and Kathe Bartlett in 1983. Nestled in a quiet wooded setting surrounded by gardens, the tasting room allows for a relaxed appreciation of the many internationally recognized wines produced here from Maine-grown fruits.

The Bartletts make some excellent fruit wines, like Pear Dry, an exceptional lemony white wine, with great fruit flavors, but not sweet at all. Slightly oaked, it is very much like an exquisite Sauvignon Blanc. It is a shock every time we serve it to someone new to the wine. Even the biggest wine snobs are impressed by this wine (which I absolutely do blind). If Bob Bartlett were making his wine in France or Italy, he would be one of those star winemakers they make documentaries about, feted and celebrated.

"I like the science and art of wine making," said Bartlett. "It's a creative process. There's a lot of things I do that are different from other people." Undeniably, he is among the greatest of fruit winemakers. Because of Maine's harsh climate, grapes are hard to grow. The Bartletts decided to make fruit wines, and they are the premiere maker of such wines, period. And their packaging is incredible.

"The Bartlett bottles are adorned with unique labels depicting old Victorian era designs of fruit and flowers. This smart packaging contributes to the overall air of sophistication surrounding the wines," wrote wine and food journalist Abigail Ingalls. "The Bartlett wines go wonderfully with food. Some popular pairings are: Oak Dry Blueberry with assorted cheeses and herb-crusted lamb. The French Oak Pear pairs very well with pork tenderloin and parsnips or a beet and walnut salad with baby spinach and dried cranberries."

My favorite is the Bartlett Maine Estate Winery's Wild Blueberry Oak Dry Wine. I bought my first bottle intending to play a practical joke on my former brother-in-law, a massive Italophile. I had bought a lovely bottle of the Super Tuscan Antinori Tignanello IGT to accompany the osso buco Michael was going to serve, but got the blueberry to pour first as a joke. I showed the Italian bottle, placing an opened Tignanello bottle at each end of the table, but poured the local wine when no one was looking. I assumed we'd taste the wine, have a good laugh, and then move on to the Italian wine. The joke was on me when the table loved the wine. I grabbed my glass and was instantly surprised! The wine tasted much like a lovely light Chianti or Dolcetto D'Alba. We let the bottle of Italian wine stand and drained the Bartlett bottle dry.

Many years ago, friend and fellow wine writer Todd Trzaskos visited us. When I told him the best red wine north of Massachusetts was from Maine, he balked. That's when I pulled out a bottle of the blueberry. With the first sip, Todd screwed up his face. Then, at about the third sip, his eyes opened wide. He'd been expecting blueberry pie in a glass but instead discovered a big, deep red wine, with fruit up front, including blackberries, cranberries, and cassis, and a great balance of acidity and tannins. Todd was in shock. Another believer was born.

On May 9, 2011, Kevin Zraly received the James Beard Foundation's Lifetime Achievement Award. After forty years of being the world's best and most widely known wine educator, and as the author of the world's best-selling wine book, *Windows on the World Complete Wine Course*, he very much deserved the recognition. After the ceremony, a party was held at the Marriott Marquis to celebrate this achievement. Many of the biggest personalities in the wine world were there. Among the more memorable wines served were a Clos de Tart, Chambertin, two stunning Amarones (1961 and 1967), and prestigious vintage Champagnes. In all, 252 people popped a cork in Kevin's honor to establish a new Guinness World Record for simultaneously opening a bottle. There were tables filled with more than two hundred bottles of wine to taste. My eyes popped out when I discovered Bartlett Estate blueberry wine among the offerings. It was a bottle signed by the winemaker himself in 1994! To many at the event, this bottle was like a scullery maid who had somehow gotten into the ball. But to my then wife and me, it was Cinderella. A seventeen-year-old blueberry wine. We tasted it and laughed, and continued tasting. At the end of the night, it was among the bottles that remained undrained. We corked the bottle and brought it home with us.

The next day, I pulled out a Riedel glass and poured myself a glass full of the garnet-colored wine. The nose was all dried cherries and a hint of tomato, along with vanilla, saddle leather, and forest floor. The taste was true to the nose. Big cherry still came through on the palate, as well as the tomato. The acids were still solid, as were the tannins, giving the wine an excellent backbone. It begged for food. I pulled out some local cheeses and nibbled on them as I sipped the wine and savored the flavors. It was an incredible experience.

Bartlett was a trailblazer, but a whole new generation of winemakers has followed in his footsteps, making quality dry wines from fruits other than grapes—apples, pears, blueberries, peaches, rhubarb, rose hips, currants, cranberries, honeyberries, crab apples, elderberries, aronia berries, and many others—that taste and drink like fine wines. They are not sweet wines. These are quality dry wines. The category is growing. Fruit wines are not some freak event; they are attracting more believers and more attention from the media, including *The New York Times*, *Saveur*, and *Food & Wine*.

Eighteen Twenty Wines

I only discovered eighteen twenty wines recently, and it instantly became one of my favorite New England small-batch boutique wineries. I love the vibe. I love what they're making. I love the packaging and the messaging. It is a great new addition to the Eastern Seaboard. It took the teamwork of owner Amanda O'Brien and her husband, Alex Denniston (who is also the winemaker), to make this vision a reality. The winery was founded in 2015 in Portland, Maine, and hit its stride several years later. Now they are the darlings of the New England wine scene.

The winery has built its reputation on rhubarb wine, embracing a farm-to-bottle ethos. The first eye-opener for me was Victoria, named after one of the most popular varieties of rhubarb grown in Maine. It has a hint of sweetness and a tart finish. It's aromatic and refreshing.

Another favorite is the Piquenique, a bright, zesty, zippy slice of strawberry rhubarb pie in a flask. Lip-smackingly good. Not cloying. A terrific rosé! Meadow is made with a different variety of rhubarb, and backsweetened with wildflower honey locally sourced from The Honey Exchange. It's almost like an unoaked Chardonnay. And then there's Bloom, a blend of wines made from rhubarb and blueberries. Amazing color, refreshing, nice tannins from the blueberries. Off-dry, perfect for sangria!

I'm really looking forward to what the ceiling for this winery is. But the sky looks limitless at this point. A must try!

Amanda O'Brien

This is the story of a local Portland girl who made good. After graduating with a degree in communications from the University of New Hampshire, Amanda went on to become a director of marketing in the tech industry, as well as a social media maven, being the event organizer for Social Media Breakfast Maine.

Amanda started eighteen twenty wines in 2015 with a friend who had been home brewing rhubarb wine. When she tried it, she had the same reaction everyone else does when they have it: "This actually tastes good."

"My friend wanted to bring it to market, so we worked together to figure out how. We started scoping out commercial spaces, then I opened the production facility and tasting room." And thus eighteen twenty wines was born. "Now, I'm just trying to grow the production to meet the demand. It's a good problem to have, but it still causes some sleepless nights."

Why rhubarb? "Rhubarb is a low-maintenance crop. It's also a spring crop, the first to come up, so what I've heard from the farmers I work with is that it's a really great crop for them, it grows off to the side and harvests in a 'shoulder season' between the summer and the fall harvests. The motivation now is getting more farmers growing rhubarb—and getting more rhubarb at the farms we're currently working with."

Their strawberry rhubarb, Piquenique, has been a big hit, even with men. "The beer bros love it," O'Brien said. "They like all the fruity beers, so why not?"

She has taken her love of wine and Maine, marketing experience, and constant curiosity to keep eighteen twenty growing. Making wine in New England has its challenges. "Each winery is run so differently, but one thing is for sure: They are all run with grit."

Bluet

According to the Bluet website, "Thoreau called wild blueberries 'bluets' and wrote of their 'innocent ambrosial taste, as if made of the ether itself.' Bluet Wild Blueberry Sparkling Wine captures summer in Maine with the purity of a single ingredient: native Maine wild blueberries." And it has received raves from Eric Asimov in *The New York Times*, Astrid Lium in *The Boston Globe*, Mary Pols in the *Portland Press Herald*, and Ray Isle in *Food & Wine*.

The wine comes in two styles: Champagne method and charmat method. Both are made from 100 percent Maine wild blueberries. With the Champagne method, secondary fermentation occurs in the bottle, followed by disgorging à la volée to expel the yeast. With the charmat method (as with Prosecco), the secondary fermentation takes place in the tank prior to filling the bottles. The wines are very different, but both are exceptional. The Champagne method boasts a fine, creamy mousse and complex flavor, while the charmat method is brightly bubbly, with a vivid fresh-berry aroma. No matter the method, this wine is as sophisticated as it is enjoyable. A great treat.

Hermit Woods Winery

Hermit Woods is an impressive winery in New Hampshire. According to their website: "Old world character meets new world fruit—each of our award-winning and handcrafted wines is made from a unique combination of locally sourced fruit, honey, and flowers, in some cases wild foraged. Our process is devotedly hands-on from vine to bottle, using old world techniques with the highest level of care and integrity."

The winery is named for Joseph Plummer, born in Londonderry in 1774, who became known as the hermit of Meredith Woods. The winery is run by the überfascinating Bob Manley (marketing), Ken Hardcastle (wine-maker), and Chuck Lawrence (finance), all of whom seem to share a love of motorcycles, sailing, and flying.

The two things you need to know about Hermit Woods are that it is one of the best wineries in New England, and that not one of the wines produced there is made from grapes.

Hermit Woods Petite Blue is a blueberry wine made from lowbush blueberries sourced from Merrill Blueberry Farms in Hancock, Maine. They use a cold-soak process to get more color and flavor, followed by a partial carbonic fermentation (a whole-berry approach) at low temperatures to extract as much flavor and fruit as they possibly can. This reductive process makes for a quality dry red wine. These are techniques Napa vintners have been using for years that Hardcastle now aims at other fruit. The wine is Rhône-ish in style, medium bodied, with blueberry, plum, and cherry and nice notes of vanilla and spice. In 2014, Ray Isle, executive wine editor of *Food & Wine*, shared a bottle with Kathie Lee Gifford and Hoda Kotb on *TODAY*. They loved it, and you will too!

Then there's Hermitage, their Bordeaux-style dark red wine. According to Ken Hardcastle, "The blackberry wine was fermented with Lalvin D254 yeast, a strain originally captured from a Rhône ferment of Syrah grapes. The blueberries were fermented with Lalvin GRE yeast (also a Rhône strain), and the elderberries with Lalvin BM 4×4, which is a proprietary blend of yeasts ideal for reds." The wine is aged in new French oak. This wine is deep, with great stewed dark fruits, spice, tannins, and acidity. Balanced and wonderfully complex.

Lake House White is a beautiful, well-balanced European-style white, with notes of French oak. Drinks like a lovely white blend. No one would believe it's not made from grapes.

Some absolutely amazing things are going on at Hermit Woods. You must get there. No excuses!

Haskap Berries

Haskap berries, also known as honeyberries, are the edible blue fruit of a particular species of honeysuckle indigenous to Canada, Russia, and Japan. They basically look like oblong blueberries. Two Canadian wineries produce very good haskap berry wines.

The Coopérative forestière du Nord-Ouest ltée operates NOASKA in New Brunswick. I love their Baker Buck Majestic Red Wine. It is an exceptional dry red wine, aged in 100 percent oak barrels. It offers notes of cassis, cocoa, and spice, layers of flavor, great tannins, and impressive complexity. A spicy finish helps the fruit last a long time. A stunning wine.

Yukon Wines, in Whitehorse, created Haskap Dry Wine, a red wine with notes of smoke and fruit. The wine is put through a cool fermentation, developing rich color and complex flavors that feature fresh cherries and hints of violets, tannins, and black pepper. Lovely, light acidity balances to make a velvety, award-winning red wine.

Maquam Barn & Winery

Maquam Winery is located in Milton, Vermont, on the northeastern shore of Lake Champlain, and is owned by Shaun Brooks. The Brooks family has been in the wine, beer, and spirits business since Prohibition, and their connection to the farm dates back to the 1600s. In 2017, they began making wine from syrup sourced in Vermont, and currently have dedicated about seven of their ten acres to the production of fruit wines. The wines are made by veteran industry consultant Dominic Rivard, an award-winning commercial winemaker and author of *The Ultimate Fruit Winemaker's Guide*. Zack Hall is the boots-on-the-ground winemaker and another industry veteran, having worked in wineries in California, France, and Quebec.

The best of their offerings is the Maquam Pear Wine, with a nose full of pear and tropical fruits, reminiscent of a fine Chardonnay or Sauvignon Blanc. Überimpressive. You can easily pass this off to the most discerning wine geek. It's delicious and stunning, wonderfully complex, and extremely balanced.

Maquam Black Currant Wine is made with 100 percent estate-grown fruit from the Green Mountains of Vermont and locally sourced Vermont grade A maple syrup. Aged in French oak for ten months, it's a dark garnet—colored dry wine, with all the big fruit you would expect up front; black and red cassis come through as promised, with a rounded, subtle tartness and impressive layers of cocoa and vanilla, caramel and spice.

White Silo Farm & Winery

White Silo is a microwinery located in Sherman, Connecticut. All of their wines are produced from their own farm-grown fruit. There aren't any 300-gallon fermentation bins, no oak barrels for aging, no fancy corking or bottling machinery. In fact, there are no grapes.

My favorite is White Silo Rhubarb Wine. A light white, very tasty, and one of the better rhubarb wines I have ever had. It has lovely tropical and melon flavors, with a citrus acidity on the finish. A distinctive white.

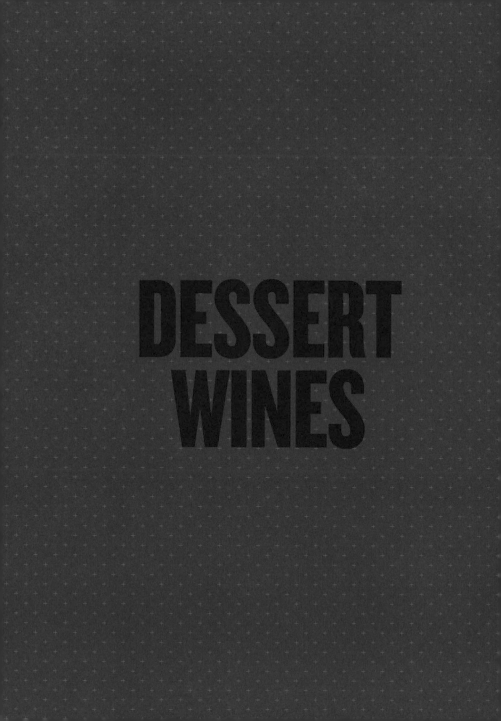

DESSERT WINES

My first great tasting experience with a dessert wine was Quady Winery's Essensia, an Orange Muscat that completely blew me away. I was working in Philadelphia, living in New Jersey, and just starting to buy wines, some to drink, some to cellar. My habit in those days, on Friday nights, was to begin my commute home by crossing over the Ben Franklin Bridge, then shooting off to Collingswood and Cherry Hill, where there were two major wine stores. One was supermarket sized, the other less than half that size but crammed to the rafters. Both offered inexpensive wines as well as more elusive, precious wines.

I had a Champagne palate but a beer wallet. I would shop carefully, measuring out how much money I could afford to spend that week. One good bottle (usually pricey, but not always) and a couple of less expensive bottles. A French white, an Italian red, a California Cabernet Sauvignon, a New Zealand Sauvignon Blanc. These were the heady late 1990s and early 2000s.

Essensia first made news in the early 1980s. I had read about it in *Wine Spectator* in the late 1990s. One night, I finally found a bottle of it and tucked it in my basket. I floated out of the store, I was so happy.

Upon my arrival home, as was my habit, I stashed the wines near the basement door. Then I burst into the house, explaining my late arrival (traffic, a late meeting with the boss, a drink with a colleague). You see, my then wife, Dominique, did not approve of my wine spending habits. But she did like fine wines. On Saturday morning, I would creep down to the basement while everyone was still asleep or groggy, unlock the door, and bring in my loot, putting it in a closet I had converted into a "wine cellar." And when asked, "Where did this new bottle come from?"

I would say we'd had it for quite some time, pretending to wipe dust from the shoulders of the bottle. I doubt she ever believed me, but was willing to let the fiction slide, as long as the wine was good.

I had purchased the bottle of Essensia for a dinner with friends. We offered a cheese course after the main meal—a cheddar, something more exotic (maybe a blue), and a brie. Fig jam—and a brown bread with walnuts and raisins.

Essensia is something different. First, the wine is clear orange, but it is not an orange wine in the sense we mean today. The wine is made by Quady Winery in Madera, California, in the San Joaquin Valley. Founded by Andrew and Laurel Quady, it specializes in dessert wines. In 1975 they released their first wine, 1,600 cases of a Zinfandel Port. In 1979 Andrew discovered an unused vineyard of Moscato Fior d'Arancio (the Italian name for what we in the US call Orange Muscat). Essensia was born of this discovery. By 1984 their business took off, and Quady has made its mark as one of the better dessert wine producers in the United States.

There are more than two hundred varieties of Muscat grapes around the world. Some experts think the grape dates to ancient Egyptian times. The origins of Orange Muscat are murky, but currently there are plantings in California, Oregon, and Australia. It is a white grape with an orange tinge. The wine is orange in color and super aromatic, with notes of orange blossoms, apricot, and honey.

My dinner guests wrinkled their noses while examining the wine's color. What kind of wine had I brought out this time? Their expressions soon changed. The wine was exquisite! Sweet, delicate, bursting with flavor, with a nice touch of acidity. And it paired beautifully with the cheese and bread and jam. I was a hero and a genius!

Dessert wines are an important part of the wine world, and if you're not exposing yourself to their incredible deliciousness, you're cheating yourself. Hunker down with a good aged Manchego or Gouda, and try an ice wine or a late harvest wine, and discover a whole new level of enjoyment. Truly, there is nothing so romantic as sharing a bottle of dessert wine with a lovely food pairing and some candlelight.

There are many dessert wines out there, for all types of folks and seasons. I will admit, the fall and winter seem to be best suited for such things. Having hosted Thanksgiving, Christmas, and New Year's for almost two decades, there was nothing more fun for family or friends than pulling out two or three of these bottles and opening them up for people to serve themselves. Give it a try!

PORT AND PORT-STYLED WINES

Port wine, a red wine fortified with neutral grain spirits, is made in the Douro region of Portugal. The name derives from the major shipping city of Porto. While primarily a sweet red wine, it is also made in dry, semidry, and white styles.

The classic food pairing for Port is crusty bread and some kind of blue cheese (but not Gorgonzola; that goes best with dry Italian reds like Barolo, Chianti, and Amarone). My choice is a blue Stilton, which has a very buttery note to it.

In Portugal, there are four grapes that go into Port. In the US, there are no rules, so Port-styled wines are made from a number of different grape varieties. There are two popular Port styles, Ruby and Tawny. Ruby is more fruit forward, with lots of dark berry flavors. Tawny has some of those flavors but also more caramel, toffee, raisin, date, and fig flavors behind it, usually due to aging.

Ruby Port

I love making Port. I was lucky enough to be invited to become the interim winemaker at Unionville Vineyards in New Jersey, which has long made one of my favorite Port-styled wines in the country. You should also try Unionville Vineyards' legendary Vat Series Port. The wine is made from a solera of 72 barrels of Chambourcin wine dating back two decades, which makes for an incredible Port wine experience. Whether you're climbing barrels or forklifting among the barrels, it takes days to get samples to start making each year's blend. A serious tasting panel takes place with as many as four or five staff members, including the general manager. Various samples of different blends are made and allowed to rest for a week or two before the final tasting and decision-making. This artfully assembled wine is incredible and unique. Some recent blends have pulled from almost twenty different years. The newest vintages offer fresh fruit, while the middle years add more muted flavors like chocolate and mocha. The oldest vintages supply sweet dates and figs. The final product has layer upon layer of flavor.

From Napa Valley, I love Madrigal Family Petite Sirah Port, Brown Estate Vineyards' Duppy Conqueror NV Port, St. Amant Winery's Bootleg Port, Pedroncelli Four Grapes Vintage Port, and Prager Winery & Port Works Club Reserve Napa Valley Port. Prager is to Port what Quady is to lighter-styled dessert wines. They are two wineries dedicated to dessert wines, and two of the top producers on the continent.

Missouri offers Ruby-styled Ports such as Mount Pleasant Estates Vintage Port, Balducci Vineyards Time Signature Release Two (a blend of

80 percent Norton and 20 percent Chambourcin), and Stone Hill Winery Port (Norton grapes).

Llano Estacado Winery Reserve Port, from Lubbock, in the Texas Highlands, is something very special.

On the East Coast, in New York there is Miles Wine Cellars Treasure Port from the Finger Lakes, made from aged Cabernet Franc. Also from the region is Lakewood Vineyards Port. Arrowhead Spring Vineyards Lockport Red is from the Niagara Escarpment. All three are quite impressive. Fox Run Vineyards Ruby Port, made from Cabernet Franc, is unctuous and sultry. From the Hudson Valley, there is Tousey Winery's The Mentor, which is full of character, as is Warwick Valley Winery's Winston's Harlequin Port.

From the mid-Atlantic, Maryland offers Boordy Vineyards Veritas, aged seven years, made from estate Chambourcin and Syrah with a touch of Petit Verdot from Washington, and Harford Vineyard & Winery Ruby Reserve. Also very special is Port of Leonardtown Winery's The Port of Leonardtown, made from Chambourcin. Cape May Winery & Vineyard on the south Jersey Shore has an extensive Port wine library. Their Isaac Smith Port is an absolute knockout.

Virginia offers impressive Ruby selections, including Stinson Vineyards Imperialis, made from Tannat, and King Family Vineyards 7, produced from 100 percent Petit Verdot. Both are incredible. Fabbioli Cellars Royalty, made in Leesburg, in Loudoun County, uses Tannat.

Also something special is a style of Port called Vin Doux, which is grape juice with just enough neutral grain spirits added to stop fermentation.

This is an ancient dessert-wine method. Fermentation is started, but then alcohol is added to stop it. The technique is called mutage and is similar to the process used to make Port. Two exceptional versions are Ankida Ridge Vineyards' Vin Doux from Virginia and Cellardoor Winery's Vin Doux Naturel, from Maine, made with 88 percent Marquette.

Tawny Port

Good Ports leave a little headspace in the barrel during aging. For Tawny Ports, a lot more headspace is usually left. With the high alcohol of the wine, this results in faster aging and contributes to the color of the wine. It also adds some of the characteristic features of Tawny, namely a nuttiness with the flavors of caramel and toffee, figs and dates.

FOX RUN VINEYARDS
FINE OLD TAWNY
FINGER LAKES
PORT

20% ALC/VOL

Fox Run Vineyards Fine Old Tawny Port from the Finger Lakes is the brainchild of Peter Bell, who created a unique aging apparatus to perfect his Tawny Port, a heated wine incubator. These barrels average anywhere from eight to ten years old in his superheated Tawny-making hive. The room is heavily insulated and stocked with the fortified barrels and several oil radiators. The room is kept at a constant temperature of 85 to 90 degrees Fahrenheit. While the wine suffers some heavy losses to the "angels' share," the resulting wine is unctuous and super complex.

Great Tawny Ports from California include Joseph Phelps Vineyards Delice Scheurebe (Napa), Ficklin Vineyards Aged 10 Years Tawny Port from Madera, and St. Amant Amador County Tawny Port. Missouri offers

Augusta Winery's Fine Old Tawny Port, aged five years, which uses the traditional solera method.

Haak Winery Reserve Tawny Port Wine out of Texas is made by Tiffany Farrell. Haak is in the nation's top tier of dessert wine houses, offering some of the best Madeira-styled wines. Winemaker Tim Benedict oversees the best Sherry-styled solera in North America, where he offers Hazlitt 1852 Vineyards Solera Sherry, out of the Finger Lakes.

LATE HARVEST WINES

Late harvest wine is made from grapes that have been left on the vine longer than usual, so that they are somewhat desiccated or raisin-y when picked, so there's less water inside the grape than at a regular harvest. Thus, the grape, though smaller, has a much higher concentration of sugar. These wines exude aroma and flavor, as well as good acidity, and tend to be sweet, but not as sweet as ice wines (more on those in a bit). They are golden in color and have the aromatics of apricots, tangerines, melon, and all manner of tropical fruit. I recommend sipping these as you enjoy a cheese course, which is where they shine. The sharpness and high fat content of the cheese provide a juxtaposition to the high sugar and acidity of the wine.

In North America, there is no more successful—and delicious—late harvest wine than Far Niente's Dolce Napa Valley Late Harvest Wine. Like the famous Sauternes of France, this wine is made from a combination of Sémillon and Sauvignon Blanc grapes. As they sit on the vines deep into the harvest, they become infected with *Botrytis cinerea*, known as noble rot. While disease is something that most winemakers fight all season long, this particular mold creates a certain richness and texture that help create the unique profile of such wine. This wine is truly at a world-class level, and would be a standout in any region. It is unctuous and rich and powerful, but also delicate, complex, and well-balanced. Its nose is a giant bouquet of floral notes, tropical notes, citrus notes, and honey.

Another wine that compares beautifully is Barboursville Vineyards Virginia Paxxito Passito. The wine is made from Moscato Ottonel and Vidal Blanc, using the classic European passito method, which allows the grapes to air-dry and "raisinize" on open racks. Excess water is drained away during the process, which concentrates the sugars. This Virginia winery—owned by the Gianni Zonin, heir to a family wine business in Italy that dates back to 1821, pulls off a minor miracle. The wine is a cunning, floral dessert bomb, rich with exotic fragrances and silky smooth fruit, finishing with a lovely acidity that keeps the wine lip-smacking. Virginia also has Linden Late Harvest Petit Manseng, and Michigan proffers Blustone Vineyards Late Harvest Riesling.

California has some notable late harvest wines, such as Napa Valley's Duckhorn Vineyards Knights Valley Late Harvest Sauvignon Blanc, Frank Family Vineyards Late Harvest Chardonnay, and Grgich Hills Estate Violetta Late Harvest. From Sonoma, there are Covenant Winery's Zahav Late Harvest Chardonnay Sonoma Mountain, Sonoma-Cutrer Russian River Late Harvest Chardonnay, and Chalk Hill Estate Selection Botrytised Sémillon.

From Washington State, look for Kiona Vineyards Columbia Valley Late Harvest Riesling, Chateau Ste. Michelle Ethos Reserve Late Harvest Riesling, Airfield Estates Late Harvest Moscato, Dunham Cellars Late Harvest Riesling, Hard Row to Hoe Vineyards Happy Ending Late Harvest Gewürztraminer, and Hogue Cellars Late Harvest Riesling. And I love the trio of wines from Oregon's Erath Winery: Sweet Harvest Pinot Blanc, Sweet Harvest Pinot Gris, and Sweet Harvest Pinot Noir.

In New York, the Finger Lakes dominate with Hermann J. Wiemer Vineyard Riesling Late Harvest, Dr. Konstantin Frank Bunch Select Late Harvest Riesling, Anthony Road Wine Company Late Harvest Vignoles, Swedish Hill Winery Late Harvest Vignoles, and Hunt Country Vineyards Late Harvest Vignoles. Long Island also has some lovely offerings: Wölffer Estate Diosa Late Harvest (a stunning late harvest Chardonnay), Paumanok Riesling Late Harvest and their Sauvignon Blanc Late Harvest, and Duck Walk Vineyards Aphrodite (a delicate late harvest Gewürztraminer).

In Canada, from the Ontario region, there are Vineland Estates Winery Select Late Harvest Riesling and their Select Late Harvest Vidal, Thirty Bench Special Select Late Harvest Vidal, Peller Estates Trius Showcase Late Harvest Vidal, Konzelmann Estate Winery Gewürztraminer Late Harvest Reserve, and Flat Rock Cellars Late Harvest Gewürztraminer, among others. Quebec offers several that I like, most notably Vignoble du Marathonien Vendange Tardive Late Harvest, made from Vidal Blanc. Two of my favorites from the Okanagan Valley are Sperling Vineyards Organic Late Harvest Vidal and Bench 1775 Whistler Late Harvest Riesling.

ICE WINE

Ice wine is made using grapes that have frozen while still on the vine. These grapes are usually harvested in the winter months. The small percentage of liquid still within the grape is usually super highly concentrated and very sugary. The grapes are pressed frozen so that only the most unctuous juices are extracted. From this the wine is made. Riesling and Vidal Blanc are most often chosen for these wines, since they have great aromas and flavors and high acidity, which ensures that the finished wine will be balanced. High sugar requires high acidity—otherwise you're drinking a lollipop.

My first taste of these wines was an Inniskillin Vidal Icewine in the late 1990s. Walter Hainle and his son Tilman made the first ice wine in Canada, a Riesling, at Hainle Vineyards Estate Winery in the Okanagan Valley in 1973, though the wines were not commercially released until 1978. For almost twenty years, only Hainle Vineyards Estate Winery and St. Laszlo Estate Winery in the Similkameen Valley offered such wines. By 1983 and 1984, a few Niagara region winemakers were attempting them, such as Hillebrand, Inniskillin, and Reif. In 1991, Inniskillin, led by Donald Ziraldo and Karl Kaiser, won the Grand Prix d'Honneur of Canada for their 1989 release of the wine. From there, Canadian ice wine skyrocketed in popularity.

Inniskillin Vidal Icewine is among the best in North America, and Canada continues to be a leader in this category, though wineries in the US have brought forth some excellent ones as well. There are rules by which a wine can be called an ice wine. In Austria, Germany, the US, and Canada, the grapes must be frozen naturally, on the vine or in the vineyard. Some winemakers resort to cryoextraction, harvesting the grapes at an opportune moment in the vineyard and then freezing them in large freezer warehouses, as is done with apples, until they press them frozen. These wines taste just like ice wines but are not allowed to use the "ice wine" designation.

Some wonderful ice wines from Canada include Jackson-Triggs Niagara Estate Reserve Vidal Icewine, Château des Charmes Vidal Icewine, Peller Estates Signature Series Cabernet Franc Icewine and their Private Reserve Vidal Icewine (Riesling, Cabernet Franc, and Vidal versions are available), Inniskillin Icewine Cabernet Franc, and Henry of Pelham Vidal Icewine.

The Finger Lakes also produce some nice ice wines, such as Hunt Country Vineyards Vidal Blanc Ice Wine, Atwater Vineyards Celsius Ice Wine, Fulkerson Winery Niagara Ice Wine, Arrowhead Spring Vineyards Vidal Blanc Ice Wine, Lamoreaux Landing Vidal Ice, and Fox Run Vineyards Hedonia Traminette. Sheldrake Point Cabernet Franc Ice Wine, a red ice wine, is also surprisingly good!

Other worthwhile American ice wines include Unionville Vineyards Cool Foxy Lady from New Jersey; Gervasi Vineyard Sognata Vidal Blanc Ice Wine from Ohio, and Presque Isle Wine Cellars Eskimo Kisses from Pennsylvania. From Michigan, there is Black Star Farms A Cappella Ice Wine, while Colorado offers Garfield Estates Vin De Glace (made with Moscato Ottonel), Whitewater Hill Vineyards Zero Below (from Viognier), and Grande River Vineyards Ice Wine. From the West Coast, my go-to is Kiona Ice Wine Red Mountain AVA Chenin Blanc.

ICE CIDER

Ice cider (also marketed as apple ice wine) works under the same general principles as ice wine, but using apples. These dessert wines are every bit as fantastic as their grape counterparts. Christian Barthomeuf, a Quebecois winemaker, is thought to be the "father of ice cider." He began his attempts in 1989, and by 1994 he was working with François Pouliot at the cidery La Face Cachée de la Pomme to create larger, more commercial runs of the product. It was a hit.

I have been to La Face Cachée de la Pomme, and no one takes their ice ciders more seriously than they do. They are world-class and stand tall next to any dessert wine from around the world. Neige Apple Ice Wine (neige means snow) is made from apples harvested in the fall and pressed at Christmastime. It smells like fresh apple juice but is thick and unctuous, with notes of dried apricot and honey, and with a lovely, zippy acidic finish. Domaine Pinnacle Quebec Ice Cider, Domaine Lafrance Ice Cider, and Union Libre Ice Cider are all tasty.

Eden Heirloom Blend Ice Cider from Vermont is incredible, and Essence from Eve's Cidery in New York is a must try.

FRUIT WINES

While there are a number of good dry fruit wines (see pages 174–187) made in North America, there are also some exquisite fruit dessert wines worth trying. These are made with raspberries, cherries, blueberry, and other fruits, with the same quality and care as other good dessert wines, and are sophisticated wines that pair well with a cheese plate.

New England is a wonderful producer of such wines. Cellardoor Winery Treasure is a blueberry dessert wine made from 90 percent wild Maine blueberries and sweetened with 10 percent local maple syrup. Bartlett Maine Estate Raspberry Wine and their Loganberry Wine are both excellent, well-balanced dessert wines.

New Hampshire offers a number of fruit dessert wines, including Hermit Woods Winery Deep Berry (strawberries) and their Deep Blue (honey and raspberries). Also excellent are Sweet Baby Vineyard Raspberry Wine and LaBelle Winery Blue Alchemy, a blueberry Port.

A longtime personal favorite is Fabbioli Cellars Raspberry Merlot from Virginia, as well as Montelle Winery Framboise, made from 100 percent fresh local raspberries. Don't miss Big Cork Vineyards' Big Finish Black Raspberry Port from Maryland. In Indiana, Huber Winery offers a sumptuous Raspberry Dessert Wine and several other fruit dessert wines. Samson Estates Winery Framboise Raspberry Dessert Wine from Everson, Washington, is also terrific.

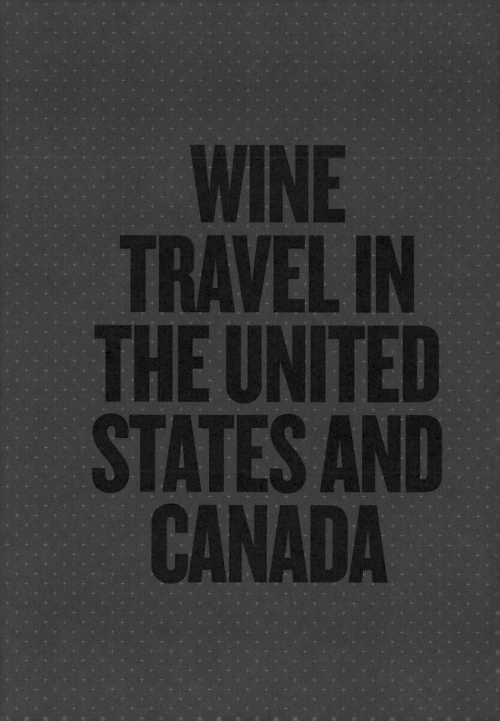

WINE TRAVEL IN THE UNITED STATES AND CANADA

Back in 2015, I was at the Edible Communities magazine publishing conference, which was held annually in Santa Barbara, California, for some time. That year, when the conference was over, I had planned one day for myself to visit some of the wineries in the region. Luckily for me, there was a massive snowstorm on the East Coast, shutting down air travel for a good 36 hours. So I rented a convertible and drove up into the hills north of Los Angeles. It was breathtaking.

I arrived at Babcock Winery at 8:15 in the morning. I found some staffers washing out stainless-steel tanks and told them I was a wine writer/publisher and fellow winery owner. I helped them finish with the tank, and they brought me into the tasting room. We talked winemaking, tasting the wines as we went along. The assistant winemaker even brought out a barrel sample of their Babcock Syrah Identity Crisis.

I learned more on that very short trip than I ever did in a classroom or at a wine tasting. I'm not suggesting those can't be or aren't learning opportunities, but travel is the best way to truly learn about wine. No substitute for it.

Since then, I've traveled to France, Italy, Spain, Chile, the West Coast, the East Coast from Maine to Virginia, and several regions in Canada. And every time I have gone forth, yes, I have enjoyed myself, but I have also learned. Here are some of my favorite places to visit.

CALIFORNIA

California is one of the most beautiful places on Earth. It doesn't seem to matter what wine region you're in, it's always a learning experience. Many of these are fully developed wine regions, with great food and wine bars galore where you can sample many wines one after the other. Doesn't matter whether you're in the northern, central, or southern regions, California has something for everyone.

Napa Valley AVA

For pure wine dopamine, nothing beats Napa Valley. Super expensive, it is the high point of American wine. Big Cabernet Sauvignon and Chardonnay. It has all the biggest names—Coppola, Mondavi, Chateau Montelena, Stag's Leap Winery, Pahlmeyer, Opus One, Duckhorn. Napa is composed of 192 square miles of vineyards. It has countless sub-AVAs, including Los Carneros, Howell Mountain, Wild Horse Valley, Stags Leap District, Mount Veeder, Atlas Peak, Spring Mountain District, Oakville, Rutherford, St. Helena, Chiles Valley, Yountville, Diamond Mountain District, Coombsville, Oak Knoll District, and Calistoga.

The good news is that there are lots of great smaller producers in Napa. Madrigal Family Winery. Ehlers Estate. Williams Selyem. William Harrison Vineyards & Winery. Hendry. Etude. Canard Vineyard. Paloma Vineyard & Winery. Paradigm Winery. Stony Hill Vineyard. The coolest urban winery in America, St. Clair Brown. Napa is always an amazing visit. And if you're a first timer, take the tour at Robert Mondavi Winery—it's the most educational wine tour in the world.

During my first visit to Napa, back in the early 1990s, on my first day there I insisted to my then girlfriend that we try to visit as many wineries as possible. I think we crashed six tasting rooms before we finally landed at Dr. Wilkinson's Backyard Resort & Mineral Springs in Calistoga, each of us already sporting massive hangover headaches. Once there, we took to the mud bath, and sank into separate giant, tiled tubs filled with steaming peat moss mud. The two gentlemen overseeing the endeavor took small shovels and loaded us up until only our heads poked out above the simmering soil.

No sooner had we settled in than I began to sweat. I felt awful. It was like being in *Alien*. I begged the attendant for water. A thickset man with a mustache shook his head in the negative. "Oh, you ran around drinking that cheap wine all day," he said, chuckling. "You gonna sweat it out now, my friend." And he was right. By the time they dug us out and showered us off, like Charlton Heston in *Planet of the Apes*, I was no longer hungover. We even shared a bottle of wine for dessert. It was magic.

Sonoma Valley AVA

Sonoma today is what Napa was twenty years ago, when it still had that country feel. Love the Cabernet Sauvignon and Chardonnay and some of the Pinot Noirs and Syrahs. There are the big places, like Benziger Family Winery, Buena Vista Winery, Gloria Ferrer, B.R. Cohn Winery, Gundlach Bundschu Winery, and Iron Horse Vineyards. Artisanal wineries include Hanzell, Peay, St. Francis, Kistler, Schermeister, Scribe, SUTRO, Fort Ross, Dutton, Kelley & Young, Clarice Wine Company, Domaine Della, and Zialena. I love Sonoma—it's one of the best regions in America.

Paso Robles AVA

Paso Robles is an oddity in that it is halfway between San Francisco and Los Angeles. It kind of gets lost in people's consciousness, being the middle child. But it is also much larger than most people realize. There are eleven sub-AVAs in the region, and more than 160 tasting rooms. Robert Hall. Turley Wine Cellars. Austin Hope. Eberle. Daou. Tablas Creek. JUSTIN. J. Lohr. Adelaida. Dunning. J Dusi. And so many more. A great region that is so much fun.

Santa Barbara County

This is one of my absolute favorite wine regions. I love their Pinot Noirs, Syrahs, and Grenaches. There are seven AVAs within the county: Santa Maria Valley, Alisos Canyon, Santa Ynez Valley, Sta. Rita Hills, Los Olivos District (which is its own thing, in my opinion), Happy Canyon of Santa Barbara, and Ballard Canyon (these last four are actually subregions of Santa Ynez Valley). Au Bon Climat. Andrew Murray Vineyards. Babcock. Beckmen. Brewer-Clifton. Byron. Carhartt Family Wines. Fess Parker. Foley. Foxen. Hartley-Ostini Hitching Post Wines. Jaffurs Wine Cellars. Kessler-Haak. Koehler. Longoria Wines. Sanford. Sea Smoke. These are just the tip of the iceberg. Great wines from this cool-climate region. This place is heaven.

While you are in Santa Barbara, be sure not to miss the Lompoc Wine Ghetto. It is an assemblage of small wine production and tasting facilities located in the Sobhani Industrial Park, directly behind the local Home

Depot. It is not picturesque in the least, but there are nineteen tasting rooms! Ampelos Cellars, Fiddlehead Cellars, Flying Goat Cellars, and Zotovich Vineyards, just to name a few. Make a day of it! Or two!

Another do-not-miss in the region is Los Olivos, a small town located in the Santa Ynez Valley. At one time, Los Olivos consisted only of a gas station, a deli, a liquor store, four or five dozen homes, and some assorted small shops. Now almost every winery has a tasting room. Wine aficionados park their cars, and the fun begins. You can stroll the sidewalks and choose from more than forty tasting rooms, as well as small boutiques, restaurants, and cafes. And yes, the gas station is still there, as well as the deli and liquor store. One of the great day visits in all of wine tourism!

Temecula Valley AVA

I had already been to the Santa Barbara wine country several times, and I thought it was time to visit the wine country northeast of the Newport Beach area in southern L.A., Temecula Valley. There is no question that this small but significant region produces lots of good Syrah and Cabernet Franc, and a solid complement of Italian grape—based wines. The Zinfandels from this region are also very good. The reds are more medium bodied than their Napa or Sonoma brethren, with bright cherry flavors and slightly more acidity. I found them surprisingly intriguing. My favorite producers include Mount Palomar, Wilson Creek, Doffo, Chapin Family Vineyards, Lorenzi Estate, Leoness Cellars, Callaway, Baily, Longshadow Ranch, and South Coast Winery, among others.

WASHINGTON AND OREGON

One of the greatest wine-traveling experiences I ever had was driving through the wine regions of Washington and Oregon. The landscapes are spectacular. Both states feature very modern port-side cities, like Seattle and Portland, with much to offer. And the wine country is inspiring. Whether you're in Willamette or Walla Walla, there is a ton to see and taste. An incredible journey and well, well worth it.

Walla Walla AVA

To me, Walla Walla is the Los Olivos of the Northwest. The town is in the more-or-less southeast corner of Washington State. A small community, it is filled with restaurants and tasting rooms. There are more than 120 wineries in the Walla Walla region. I literally wanted to move there after I first visited. I like Walla Walla because they grow everything from Albariño to Viognier, from Cabernet Franc to Zinfandel. And it all seems to come out beautifully. Some of my favorite wineries are L'Ecole No. 41, Gård, DAMA, Bledsoe Family Winery, Doubleback,

Garrison Creek Cellars, Helix Wines, Leonetti Cellar, Long Shadows, Reininger, and many more. A terrific region filled with exceptional wine. You'll put lots of miles on your car traveling from one large farm to the next. A lovely agricultural region.

Yakima Valley AVA

A subregion of the Columbia Valley AVA in central Washington State, the Yakima wine region is composed of six AVAs: Naches Heights, Yakima Valley, Rattlesnake Hills, Snipes Mountain, Red Mountain, and Horse Heaven Hills. The most grown grape varieties there include Chardonnay, Riesling, Merlot, and Cabernet Sauvignon, yet the region is far more diverse than that. Yakima is the oldest AVA in the state, established in 1983. The oldest Cabernet Sauvignon vines were planted as far back as 1963, at Harrison Hill Vineyard.

I spent a week driving around Yakima and loved every minute of it. If you like farms, farmers, and farming, you'll love Yakima. It's still very much an agricultural region. The wines are impressive, and the people very down-to-earth. I loved wineries like Kana Winery, Betz Family, De-Lille Cellars, Andrew Will, Succession Wines, Drum Roll Wine, Cairdeas Winery, Dineen Vineyards, J Bell Cellars, Chateau Ste. Michelle, Two Mountain, VanArnam, 14 Hands, and Hedges Family Estate, among many others.

Willamette Valley AVA

For pure beauty, the Willamette (pronounced like Janet) Valley in Oregon is hard to beat. There are more than seven hundred wineries there, across 3.4 million acres. It is home to eleven sub-AVAs, including Chehalem Mountains, Dundee Hills, Eola–Amity Hills, Laurelwood District, Lower Long Tom, McMinnville, Ribbon Ridge, Tualatin Hills, Van Duzer Corridor, Yamhill-Carlton, Mount Pisgah, and Polk County, Oregon. Hills and farms blanket this region—it's as picturesque as it gets. The region grows more than a hundred different varieties of grapes and makes great Riesling, Pinot Gris, Pinot Noir, Chardonnay, Syrah, and Cabernet Sauvignon.

Some of my favorite wineries include The Four Graces, Abacela, Stoller Family Estate, Sokol Blosser, Brooks Wine, The Eyrie Vineyards, Troon, Durant, Adelsheim, Erath, Domaine Drouhin, Ken Wright Cellars, Pudding River, and Denison Cellars. The Willamette is an exceptional place to visit.

NEW YORK

New York is home to America's oldest winery (Brotherhood Winery) and the oldest continuously farmed vineyards (the old Caywood Vineyards, now at Benmarl). But that's just the beginning. New York is a state of diversity. There are three major regions, and each is completely different—the Finger Lakes with its stunning vistas, the giant waterway that is the historic Hudson River, and the beautiful sandy landscapes of Long Island. Each region could not be more different, and all are excellent.

Finger Lakes AVA

Visiting the Finger Lakes region is like driving through the Italian lake country, but with Victorian houses and some Mennonites thrown in. Farmers markets. Big lakes. Rolling hills covered with grapes. Absolutely spectacular. There are five subregions and wine trails within the Finger Lakes. It is one of the truly great Riesling regions of the world, and also produces flavorful Gewürztraminer, Blaufränkisch, Pinot Noir, and Cabernet Franc. There are some incredible wine-makers there, like Nancy Irelan, Nova Cadamatre, Peter Becraft, Nathan Kendall, Kelby James Russell, and Ian Barry. The list goes on. Favorite wineries include Heart & Hands Wine Company, Trestle 31, Nathan K. Finger Lakes Wines, Red Newt Cellars, Billsboro, Red Tail Ridge, Anthony Road, Scout, Barry Family Cellars, Hermann J. Wiemer, Fox Run, Dr. Konstantin Frank Winery, Ravines Wine Cellars, Weis, Shaw, Forge Cellars, Boundary Breaks, and the Voleur label (at Montezuma) and Local Culture label (at Idol Ridge), both from winemaker Phil Plummer. Lots of wonderful restaurants and great scenery.

North Fork of Long Island AVA

This is one of the older AVAs on the East Coast and among the most developed. More than forty wineries pack the North Fork (with three on the South Fork, in Southampton). Great Cabernet Franc, Malbec, Merlot, Chardonnay, and Sauvignon Blanc. Love Bedell Cellars, Macari, Lenz, Paumanok, McCall, Roanoke, Pellegrini, Saltbird Cellars, Terra Vite, The

Old Field Vineyards, Harbes, Sparkling Pointe, Wölffer Estate, Channing Daughters, Sannino, Coffee Pot Cellars, Palmer, and Suhru, among many others. Picturesque and delicious. A lotta tan people drinking rosé in summer whites and sunglasses. Super fun!

Hudson Valley AVA

The Hudson Valley is big, extending from New York City north to just beyond Albany, and comprises the Shawangunk Wine Trail (by far the largest and oldest), the Dutchess Wine Trail, the Hudson-Berkshire Beverage Trail, and the Upper Hudson Wine Trail. The region possesses the oldest continually running winery in the United States, Brotherhood Winery, the oldest continually in-use vineyards in the country (originally Caywood Vineyards, now Benmarl), and the oldest farm wineries in the state, including Benmarl and Clinton Vineyards (now a part of Milea Vineyards). The region is also the home of the largest, most prestigious, and grandest of cooking schools, the Culinary Institute of America, which features its own brewery run by Brooklyn Brewery.

The Hudson Valley has been a hotbed of innovation. Piquettes, co-ferments, Pét Nats, and dozens of collaboration products have made the region one of the most exciting in the country. However, the distances between wineries can be daunting. Regardless, the region is also the most diverse in America. It has more craft beverage businesses than any of the other wine regions. You cannot go a stone's throw in any direction without hitting a winery, brewery, distillery, or cidery.

Some of the wineries to follow include Fjord, Benmarl, Cereghino Smith, Robibero, Whitecliff, Warwick Valley, Millbrook, Milea, Hudson-Chatham, Tousey, Victory View, Fossil Stone, and Galway Rock.

CONNECTICUT AND RHODE ISLAND

Southeastern Connecticut has three wonderful wineries, Stonington Vineyards, Jonathan Edwards Winery, and Saltwater Farm Vineyard, all in the Stonington area. There's also Sharpe Hill Vineyard in Pomfret. In Rhode Island, you must visit Greenvale Vineyards just outside of Newport, on the Atlantic coast, and Carolyn's Sakonnet Vineyard in Little Compton, on the other side of Newport Bay. This whole trip will yield amazing wines and New England charm so thick you'll have to brush it off. Promise. You will love it.

NEW JERSEY, PENNSYLVANIA & MARYLAND

These are all spread out, but there are tremendous gems hidden within them. In New Jersey, visit Alba Vineyards, William Heritage Winery, Unionville, Beneduce, Hawk Haven, Bellview, Auburn Road, and Working Dog, among many good ones. In Pennsylvania, there's Va La Vineyards (perhaps the best and least known vineyard in America, with Italian-styled blends like Silk, Cedar, and Mahogany), Galen Glen, Karamoor, ParadocX, Chaddsford, Vox Vineti, and Penns Woods. Maryland has one of the best wineries on the East Coast, Boordy Vineyards (founded by Philip Wagner, who saved winemaking on the East Coast and who followed H. L. Mencken as editor of *The Baltimore Sun*), Big Cork, Black Ankle, Old Westminster, Crow, Bordeleau, Port of Leonardtown, Harford, Thanksgiving Farm Winery, and The Wine Collective in Baltimore, among many others.

It's all too easy to make fun of these regions—cracks about "What exit?" and cheesesteaks and crabs and crime. But the simple fact is that there is great wine being made in every one of these states, and some truly surprising ones.

VIRGINIA

Virginia has more than 300 wineries, many of them excellent. The state began its long association with wine when Thomas Jefferson, a fan of Bordeaux, attempted to grow wine grapes at his home, Monticello. Fantastic Cabernet Franc, Petit Verdot, Chardonnay, and Viognier can be found there, among many others. The premiere winery in the state is Barboursville Vineyards, owned by the Italian Zonin family, which boasts the long-running team of viticulturist Fernando Franco and winemaker Luca Paschina. Their Italian varietals, their Octagon Bordeaux-style blend, and their dessert wine Paxxito are among the best in the land.

Virginia is simply one of the best wine regions on the East Coast, with some of my favorite wineries, such as Jefferson Vineyards, Keswick, King Family, Fabbioli Cellars, Walsh Family Wine, Veritas, Early Mountain, Rosemont of Virginia, Linden, Afton Mountain, RdV Vineyards, Pearmund Cellars, Fifty-Third Winery & Vineyard, Delaplane Cellars, Cardinal Point, Blenheim, Bluestone Vineyard, Narmada, Pollack, DuCard, and Ankida Ridge, among others.

MISSOURI

A lot of people don't know that some of the country's oldest wineries are located in Missouri. Augusta, Missouri, was awarded its status as the first AVA in the United States on June 20, 1980. There are 130 wineries divided into nine wine trails in the Show Me State. The Hermann Wine

Trail is just outside St. Louis; it is the most concentrated and one of the oldest. Kansas City supports three different wine trails that begin outside the city limits. There's also the Lake of the Ozarks Wine Trail. Stone Hill Winery, in Hermann, is more than 175 years old, having been established in 1847. It is the second-oldest winery in continuous operation in the United States. Traminette, Vidal Blanc, Vignoles, and Chardonel are among the most popularly planted white grapes, while Chambourcin and Norton number among the most popular reds. Pass under the St. Louis Archway, and head west out of town. A fun, fun visit. St. James, Noboleis Vineyards, Les Bourgeois Vineyards, Röbller Vineyard, Adam Putcha Winery, and Montelle are all impressive.

TEXAS

The hundred wineries in Fredericksburg and the Texas Hill Country AVA are a must visit. Although many people aren't aware of it, Texas has some tremendous producers and great wines. In Gillespie County alone, there are sixty wineries! Some of the top wineries to taste include Kuhlman Cellars, Fall Creek, Becker, Llano Estacado, Pedernales, William Chris Vineyards, Messina Hof Winery, Ron Yates Wines, Bent Oak, Limestone Terrace, and English Newsom Cellars. Most importantly, visit Haak Wines, where you'll find some of the best Port- and Madeira-styled wines in America, all made by winemaker Tiffany Farrell.

COLORADO

With more than three hundred days of sunshine per year, Colorado is a great place to grow delightful wine. Colorado offers two AVA regions: Grand Valley and West Elks. Other wine regions within the state include McElmo Canyon and Montezuma County, Surface Creek and South Grand Mesa, Fremont County near Pikes Peak, Olathe and Montrose

Counties, and the Front Range and Western Slope (the growing regions east and west of the Continental Divide, respectively). The state's top vinifera include Merlot, Cabernet Sauvignon, Syrah, and Cabernet Franc, as well as Chardonnay, Riesling, and Viognier.

Some of the wineries producing the best wines in the state include Carboy, The Winery at Holy Cross Abbey, Vino Salida Wine Cellars, Whitewater Hill, Slaymaker Cellars, Buckel Family Wine, Monkshood Cellars, Bookcliff Vineyards, Colterris (in Palisade), The Storm Cellar, Jack Rabbit Hill Farm, Carlson Vineyards, and Two Rivers Winery. For incredible sightseeing and fun driving, you can't beat Colorado.

MICHIGAN

Michigan is fast growing in its reputation for fantastic wines. There are five wine trails in the state: Lake Michigan Shore, Leelanau Peninsula, Old Mission Peninsula, Petoskey Wine Region, and Sunrise Side Wine & Hops Trail. There are almost two hundred wineries in the state.

Vinifera reds far outweigh hybrids. Pinot Noir is the biggest of the vinifera grapes, with more than 250 acres planted; it is by far their number one red varietal wine. That's followed by 170-plus acres of Cabernet Franc and more than 125 acres of Merlot. Chambourcin brings up the rear with over 79 acres planted. Surprisingly, there are only 70 acres of Marquette and 42 acres of Blaufränkisch.

Michigan's wine country is spread out, but if you get a chance, stop in to taste some of the local wines—they are shockingly good. Some wineries to be on the lookout for include Mackinaw Trail, Petoskey Farms, Shady Lane Cellars, Left Foot Charley, Domaine Berrien Cellars, Stranger Wine Company, Detroit Vineyards, St. Julian Winery, Fenn Valley, Dablon, Black Star Farms, Round Barn, Lawton Ridge, Free Run Cellars, Chateau Chantal, Chateau Fontaine, Cherry Creek Cellars, and Mawby for truly incredible sparkling.

CANADA

The Canadian wine industry is famous for its ice wines, but it also offers incredible diversity and quality. The Niagara-on-the-Lake region is as charming and beautiful as any, and their wines measure up. The Okanagan Valley is stunning. Canadian wine is a real winner, and undervalued. There is so much to discover there.

Ontario VQA

I discovered the Niagara-on-the-Lake region (a subregion of the Niagara Peninsula) in the Ontario VQA quite by accident. We were vacationing with our then small children on the American side of the Falls. I was bored silly at the indoor pool and decided I would visit a winery I had heard was just over the border. When I got to the other side, it was like arriving in Oz (albeit, it was winter, so everything was white and gray). There is a whole world there where they make exceptional Cabernet Franc, Pinot Noir, Chardonnay, and Riesling, as well as dessert wines, among other things. It is an absolutely special place, one of my favorite regions, right up there with Santa Barbara.

There are five regions in the Ontario VQA, including Prince Edward County, Lake Erie North Shore, and Niagara Peninsula. Special wineries include Tawse, Flat Rock Cellars, Vineland Estates, Château des Charmes, Southbrook Vineyards, Cave Spring, Ravine Vineyard Estate, Colaneri Estate, Henry of Pelham, Hidden Bench Estate, Inniskillin, Jackson-Triggs, Konzelmann Estate, Lailey, Peller Estates, Redstone, Reif Estate, Stratus, Sue-Ann Staff Estate, Thirty Bench, Trius, Wayne Gretzky, and more. Lovely medium-bodied reds and terrific bright whites. Super, super special.

Okanagan Valley

If you visit Vancouver, and you don't reserve a day to travel to the Okanagan Valley, then shame on you—you just missed out on one of the most charming and beautiful wine regions in North America. In fact, the Okanagan gets more sun annually than Napa Valley. It boasts eight sub-regions: Golden Mile Bench, Naramata Bench, Skaha Bench, Okanagan Falls, Lake Country, Peachland/Summerland/Penticton, Oliver, and Osoyoos. The region is known for its Chardonnay, Merlot, Syrah, and Riesling varietal wines.

Mission Hill Family Estate Winery, Covert Farms Family Estate, Arrowleaf Cellars, Frequency Wine Co., CheckMate Artisanal Winery, Painted Rock Estate, Quails' Gate Estate, Laughing Stock, Burrowing Owl Estate, Tantalus, Le Vieux Pin, Black Hills Estate, and Poplar Grove are among many of the excellent wineries in this region. It's as scenic an area as there is. Simply beautiful.

ABOUT THE AUTHOR

Carlo DeVito is one of the most experienced wine, beers, and spirits editors in the world, whose list of authors has included *The Wine Spectator*, *The New York Times*, Michael Jackson, Kevin Zraly, Clay Risen, Matt Kramer, Oz Clarke, Tom Stevenson, Howard G. Goldberg, Josh M. Bernstein, Stephen Beaumont, Ben McFarland, Jim Meehan, Salvatore Calabrase, William Dowd, and many others.

His books and authors over the years have won James Beard, Gourmand, and IAACP awards. He has traveled to wine regions in California, Canada, up and down the east coast, France, Spain, and Chile. He is the author of more than 20 books, including *Big Whiskey*, *Tennessee Whiskey*, and the *Spirit of Rye*.

ABOUT CIDER MILL PRESS BOOK PUBLISHERS

Good ideas ripen with time. From seed to harvest, Cider Mill Press brings fine reading, information, and entertainment together between the covers of its creatively crafted books. Our Cider Mill bears fruit twice a year, publishing a new crop of titles each spring and fall.

"Where Good Books Are Ready for Press"
501 Nelson Place
Nashville, Tennessee 37214

cidermillpress.com